Spiritual

formation for pastors

Spiritual

formation for pastors
FEEDING THE FIRE WITHIN

MICHAEL GEMIGNANI

JUDSON PRESS
VALLEY FORGE

Spiritual Formation for Pastors: Feeding the Fire Within

© 2002 by Judson Press, Valley Forge, PA 19482-0851

Unless otherwise marked, Bible quotations in this volume are from the New Revised Standard Version of the Bible, copyright © 1989 by the Division of Christian Education of the National Council of the Churches of Christ in the United States of America. Used by permission. All rights reserved.

Other Bible quotations are from *The Jerusalem Bible*, Copyright © 1966 by Darton, Longman & Todd, Ltd. and Doubleday and Company, Inc. Used by permission of the publisher.

Library of Congress Cataloging-in-Publication Data
Gemignani, Michael C.
   Spiritual formation for pastors : feeding the fire within / Michael Gemignani.
   p. cm.
[Includes bibliographic references.]
ISBN 0-8170-1432-2 (pbk. : alk. paper)
   1. Clergy—Religious life. 2. Spiritual formation. I. Title.

BV4011.6 .G45 2002
248.8'92—dc21   2002020521

Printed in the U.S.A.

08 07 06 05 04 03 02

10 9 8 7 6 5 4 3 2 1

To my beloved wife, Nilda

CONTENTS

FOREWORD

ADULT SPIRITUAL GROWTH IS THE KEY TO MISSION. THAT simple truth has never been articulated so glibly, and pursued so poorly, as in today's traditional churches. Children's ministries spring up quickly out of the anxiety of parents for the moral health and spiritual depth of their kids, only to flounder because the parents are unwilling to model the very disciplines they expect of their children. Youth ministries flourish for fleeting months with professional staff and infusions of capital, only to perish because adults haven't the spiritual depth to cope with the inevitable changes to cultural assumptions and congregational habits that youth demand. Congregations talk a great deal about mission, but adult members assume their only role is to raise money to pay somebody else to do it. It is time to raise the bar of expectation for serious, timely, time-consuming, energetic, partnered, and mentored adult spiritual growth.

This book takes adult spiritual growth *seriously*. Its general focus is on the spiritual growth of clergy, but do not let that deceive you. The focus is only on clergy because clergy must motivate, coach, and model serious spiritual growth for church members and new seekers alike. Everyone must become involved in the work of personal, holistic growth and discernment of Christian calling.

You know that a congregation is becoming serious about adult spiritual growth when core leaders (clergy and laity) and committed members begin to integrate and embed the insights of this book into their lifestyles. As Michael Gemignani says,

> Spirituality is that aspect of my faith that serves to guide me in how I conduct my life. It is the framework within which I operate in my desire to be faithful to God.

1. *Begin with desire.* Instill in Christian adults the craving, yearning, dreaming, thirsting desire to be with Christ, sharing in his sufferings and participating in his resurrection (Philippians 3:8-11), celebrating hope in the midst of life's struggle.

2. *Aim at behavior.* Coach Christian adults to go deep into spirituality for the sole purpose of changing their daily lifestyle and conduct, so that spiritual growth redirects their intimacy, reshapes their career, and reprioritizes their financial planning.

Adult spiritual growth is not a matter of satisfying idle curiosity about the sociology of the ancient Middle East, or about proving the existence of God, or about shaping American public policy. It is not a theological or ideological continuing education program. It is a companionship with Christ on the road to mission. It is the reenactment in your own life of the disciples' experience on the road to Emmaus, as Jesus pauses in timely fashion, with you and your peers, to ignite a fire in your hearts, open your minds, and redirect your footsteps to follow him into mission. If spirituality does not do that, it is a waste of your and God's time.

Veteran church people and weary clergy will particularly

appreciate this book, because it provides practical coaching to refocus their lives and renew their joy in Christ. It will help clergy recapture the passion of their original calling that has become lost amid operating deficits and comforting "Aunt Nelly" about her aching bunion. It helps veteran church members renew their trust in clergy to lead the church into the mysterious future, not by skillful expertise that will go out of date tomorrow, but by the authenticity of their spiritual lives and the audacity of their biblical visions.

Perhaps the best advice of all deserves to be mentioned at the very beginning. Spiritual growth is a *partnership*. Meditation and contemplation may well include opportunities for solitude, but in the end these spiritual-growth tactics will help you delve deeper and leap further only if spirituality becomes a team effort. Look for mentors in both obvious and unexpected places—and become a mentor in both predictable and surprising contexts. Grow in a triad, a small group, a covenant, or a class—but never follow Christ into mission on your own. Paul took Luke, Onesimus, Timothy, Priscilla, Lydia, and others with him. You do the same.

Thomas Bandy
March 2002

ACKNOWLEDGMENTS

I AM INDEBTED TO MY EDITOR RANDY FRAME FOR HIS PATIENT and invaluable assistance. My thanks, too, to Lillie Rowden, a dear friend, who read the initial draft of my manuscript and made a number of helpful comments and suggestions.

section 1

THE LOOK
OF A SOUND
SPIRITUALITY

SPIRITUALITY IS A "HOT TOPIC" IN THE UNITED STATES. Bookstores offer not several shelves, but several sections devoted to books on subjects that reasonably could be designated as "spiritual." One can browse the shelves in "Religion," "New Age," "Self-Help," and "Psychology" to find numerous books related to traditional Christian faith, but also numerous books on Eastern religions; finding inner peace; caring for one's soul; developing one's psychic powers; and communicating with deceased relatives, with angels, or with other beings from the spirit realm. One does not have to conduct public opinion polls to conclude that there is an interest in all things spiritual at what may well be a level unprecedented in the history of this nation.

If for no reason other than this extraordinary public interest in spirituality, pastors should be able to talk to their congregants about spirituality in general and, particularly, spirituality in the Christian tradition. It may be an indictment of contemporary Christianity that so many are seeking spiritual fulfillment outside its fold. Perhaps many of those who have turned to New Age and other non-Christian sources in their spiritual quests have tried local Christian churches and found those sources unable to fulfill their needs, even though Christian tradition is rich in guidance for those committed to a spiritual life.

But a deeper reason why spirituality must be important to Christian pastors is that without a personal spirituality, they may not be as open as they should be to God's action in their lives. They may be less likely to discern how God is moving in their lives and how to respond to that movement. And they may not be the visionary men and women of faith that God wants them to be as leaders of the people of God, the church.

We will explore the nature of spirituality in greater depth in chapter 2. Of course, different people use the term "spirituality" in different ways. For some, it is simply doing good works. For others, it is particular prayer practices. For still others, it is faith. All of these interpretations have validity in some context, but none of them provide the definition that I use in this book. We want our concept of spirituality to have practical consequences—an applicability to our lives that will bring them more in touch with God, and an applicability to our ministries that will make them more effective in spreading the kingdom. To accomplish this, spirituality, or rather, a spirituality, must be a framework on which our lives and ministries are built. It is much like the skeleton of the body. Without the skeleton, the body would collapse. But the skeleton is not the entire body; it is a scaffold, as it were, for the body.

From this, we rightly can conclude that spirituality gives structure and focus to our life in God. This structure is a valuable aid to spiritual growth for all Christians, but it is particularly useful for clergy. Clergy are, after all, leaders in the church. They are those called by God to guide their congregants into a deeper relationship with God. They are to help those entrusted to their care to grow into spiritual maturity with the help of the Holy Spirit. If the pastors do not have a strong framework on which to build their own spiritual lives, they will be less able to lead by word or by example. In addition, they risk being swayed this way and that by the latest fads rather than setting a steady, well-ordered course for their own and their church's worship and ministry.

This book is divided into two parts. In the first part, after reviewing the importance of a strong spirituality for clergy, we explore the nature of spirituality. Then we proceed from the general to the particular, moving from Christian spirituality to clergy spirituality to the spirituality of the individual pastor. The first part ends with a discussion of the signs of healthy and unhealthy spiritualities.

The second part talks about spiritual formation, that is, the development of a healthy personal spirituality. After discussing spiritual formation generally, we explore meditation, contemplation, spiritual direction, and other aids to clergy spirituality. We focus in large measure on a pattern of life founded on an intentional spirituality.

Let us begin.

1

THE NEED FOR A SOUND SPIRITUAL FOUNDATION

CLERGY FACE SPIRITUAL CHALLENGES
Brother Johnson had been pastor of the Shady View Baptist Church for thirteen years. During that time, he watched the church's neighborhood change from middle-class white to economically struggling multiethnic. Attendance at Shady View showed a steady decline over the last eight years as members of the congregation migrated to the suburbs and few of the neighborhood's new residents seemed interested in Shady View's style of worship. Brother Johnson was confused. Should he seek another church? Challenge the congregation to greater outreach in the area around the church? Just hang on for a few more years until he could retire? He no longer was sure of his vision either for himself or for Shady View.

Father Smith, an Episcopal priest for fifteen years, took a large, prosperous parish that was a considerable step up from the small, rural congregation he had just left. He soon found that he had stepped into a bitter and divisive struggle about Sunday worship. The previous rector had been "high church" and would not allow even a piano, much less a guitar, to accompany congregational singing. His services were so formal that a number of families, particularly the younger ones, began demanding that he make worship more contemporary. Father Smith could sense the pain on both sides and found that he himself was unsure of where he stood. He asked himself the question again and again, "What am I trying to accomplish during the services?"

Pastor Jones, the pastor of a Lutheran congregation, was sick at heart. The wife in a couple that she married just four years earlier had come to tell her tearfully that she was getting a divorce. Until that point, Pastor Jones had thought that the couple was getting along well, since they both regularly attended Sunday services and church-sponsored socials. To make matters worse, this was the third couple in her parish that month that was separating. That, together with two terminally ill cancer patients and a recently diagnosed victim of Alzheimer's, put more pressure on her than she thought she should have to bear. She ranted in private at God for allowing these tragedies to visit the flock entrusted to her care, but to the congregation she felt compelled by her leadership role to present a buoyant, joyful front.

Very few members of the clergy will find themselves unable to identify with Brother Johnson, Father Smith, and Pastor Jones. Very few members of the clergy would be unable to add other scenarios of clergy facing uncertainty, loneliness, emotional strain, and temptation to despair. Clergy are expected to support members of their congregations in times of need, but rarely do they feel able to express their own needs to those same congregations lest they appear weak, spiritually deficient, and incapable of aiding those who call on them for help.

Even with a strong spiritual foundation, clergy risk discouragement and burnout. Without a strong spiritual foundation, clergy are almost certain to crash and burn. Or worse, clergy without a strong spiritual foundation may treat their ministry as just another "secular" profession, applying the same techniques and standards for success that the world applies. If their congregations gain spiritual strength, it will be in spite of their leadership rather than because of it. Without a firm spiritual foundation laid by the pastor with the help of God, even a seemingly strong congregation can be destroyed by the storm of a crisis.

One Episcopal priest whom I know noted that of his seminary class of fifteen years ago, only one-third was in ministry full time, and one-third had left the ministry completely. I am certain that clergy in other denominations can cite similarly grim statistics. Why do so many men and women enter the ordained ministry with enthusiasm and a desire to serve God only to leave the active ministry, often disheartened and cynical, after just a few years? Is it due to misguided expectations of what ministry involves? Is it due to the stress on family life that ministry often brings as a pastor is torn between the care demanded by the extended family of the congregation and the care required by the immediate family of spouse and children? Is it due to a pay scale not commensurate with the level of education expected in some denominations, pay that often is insufficient to support a family? Undoubtedly, these often are factors in clergy abandoning the active ministry, but I believe that a major problem with many clergy, both those who stay and those who leave, is the lack of a strong spiritual vision for themselves and for those they serve. As Scripture says, "Without a vision, the people perish." And so do clergy.

CLERGY NEED A CLEAR SPIRITUAL VISION
Almost every member of the clergy will state that his or her top priority is to be faithful to God. Indeed, if a clergyperson is seeking personal power, job security, or prestige rather than

God's will, then that person never should have entered the ministry in the first place. So we will take it as axiomatic that clergy want to be faithful disciples of God. They want to do whatever it is that God wants them to do. Exactly what is it, however, that God wants them to do?

A common failing among Christians, lay and clergy alike, is to assume that God wants what they want. If I want to plant a church in a growing suburb, I will, of course, pray about it first, but I may decide that since to me the project looks so promising and the idea seems so appealing, God must want me to plant that church. After all, God wants me to spread the gospel wherever I can. So I make the decision and ask God to bless it, when in reality the decision primarily was my own, not God's. We all are guilty of mistaking our own will for God's will from time to time. Generally, however, we do not make that mistake out of rebelliousness but out of ignorance, because God's will is not always easy to identify.

Virtually all clergy sincerely want to know God's will, and they would follow it if they knew what it was, but often they are unable to discern what God wants. Brother Johnson, in the first example of this chapter, is genuinely unsure what God desires of him. He has three choices, none of which seems to pop out with "God's Will for You" emblazoned on it in big red letters. Father Smith is also perplexed, because he cannot discern what sort of worship God is asking of his church, and he may, in fact, see nothing that he can implement without losing a sizable number of his members. The tragedies besetting so many members of Pastor Jones's congregation are gnawing away at her vitality, and she does not think that God allows her to reveal her own weakness to those she is trying to help, and so her fidelity to what she thinks is God's will is destroying her happiness and perhaps also her effectiveness as a minister.

If the clergy themselves are confused spiritually, their congregations likely will be confused as well. As St. Paul reminds us, if the trumpet call is uncertain, the soldiers will not know what is expected of them (1 Corinthians 14:8). Clergy must have a clear spiritual vision to guide their decisions, even when God's will in specific instances is not immediately obvious. Clergy must have a strong spiritual foundation on which to build that will carry them through the crises that are sure to come, a foundation that will help them make difficult decisions when such decisions are needed. Clergy must themselves have a solid spiritual formation if they are to form their flocks spiritually.

As members of the clergy it is vital to be able to say, "Jesus is Lord," but more than that is required if we are to exercise spiritual leadership. It is crucial to have compassion for the people who are suffering and for sinners, but even that is not enough to exercise spiritual leadership. Leadership implies that the leader provides direction for those who follow—but leaders can only direct if they are themselves directed. There are many different styles by which a leader can provide that direction, but a leader who has no idea where he or she wants to go will only confuse and frustrate those whom he or she leads. Thus, the clergy must have a spiritual vision, a spirituality, that guides them so that they can guide others, and they gain and strengthen that spirituality through the process of spiritual formation.

IF CLERGY DO NOT LEAD, OTHERS WILL

Many, perhaps most, of us are familiar with situations of churches in which clergy did not provide direction. The pastor conducted services, visited the sick, preached sermons, and taught Sunday school, but did not provide leadership. He or she was simply "there," without projecting a vision to challenge the congregation to grow spiritually.

Clergy operating in this mode may try to justify it by claiming that their style is "nondirective." They want the laity to set their own direction and take responsibility for the work of the church. Although the laity should, indeed, take responsibility for the work of the church, leadership is still required. If there is no central vision communicated in whatever way by the clergy, each member of the church will develop his or her own vision or will simply opt out of participating in ministry beyond, perhaps, coming to Sunday services.

One or more strong lay leaders with firmly held views of what the church should be doing will emerge and create their own power centers. Competing factions and conflicts are almost certain to arise to threaten the unity of the congregation. As the maxim goes, "Power abhors a vacuum." We might paraphrase that saying this way: "If the presumptive leader will not lead, others will." Another grim alternative is that no leader will emerge and the church will atrophy and die.

But if the pastor cannot establish a spiritual vision for the congregation, it is unlikely that a layperson will. If the pastor does not provide the spiritual foundation on which the congregation can build, perhaps because he or she does not have such a foundation personally, the congregation will not be able to reach its own spiritual potential.

Of course, it is God who enables any individual or group to grow spiritually. The clergy are instruments of God. They can do nothing good of themselves, but depend on the sanctifying power of the Holy Spirit for genuine spiritual progress. But Christ chose to use human instruments for his work, and if those instruments are not growing spiritually, that work will suffer. If the clergy cannot or will not lead, the leadership Christ intends them to exercise in their vocations will be exercised by those who are not called by God to such leadership.

SIGNS OF A SOUND SPIRITUALITY

In later chapters we will explore spirituality and personal spiritual formation, but we might ask now, What are some of the signs of a sound spiritual foundation? Among them I would include the four that follow here.

HUMILITY Humility is nothing other than honesty about oneself. If I can write beautiful music, I should not deny that I have good musical ability or refuse to write music in order not to call attention to myself or move others to compliment me. Rather, I should use my talent in the service of God. If people compliment me, I simply thank them, silently giving praise for being allowed to love God through my compositions. Humility, coupled with an honest assessment of one's talents and use of those talents in the service of God and others, is characteristic of spiritual grounding.

COMPASSION Jesus ordered us not to judge others lest we ourselves be judged. He associated openly with the lowest social classes, even the most despised, of his society, calling some of them to be his most intimate disciples. We should have an acute sense of our own unworthiness compared to God's infinite glory and goodness and never judge ourselves to be better than others. We are to see and serve Christ in the least of our brothers and sisters, weeping with them in their sorrow, laughing with them in their joy, always reflecting the divine mercy given to us and showered on all who call on God's name. Our spiritual foundation, if it is solid, will be projected to others by the compassion of Christ that they see demonstrated in how we relate to others, particularly sinners and outcasts.

LOVE I can do no better than to quote 1 Corinthians 13: 4-7: "Love is always patient and kind; it is never jealous; love is never boastful or conceited; it is never rude or selfish; it does not take offense, and is not resentful. Love takes no pleasure in other people's sins but delights in the truth; it is always ready to excuse, to trust, to hope and to endure whatever comes" (Jerusalem Bible). Above all, spiritual maturity is characterized by the love of others according to the New Commandment, "You shall love others as you have first been loved" (see John 13:34; 15:12). In Christ, we have all been loved with a sacrificial love that was willing to give up life itself so that we might have eternal life. If our worst enemy, or most obnoxious parishioner, could come to God only through our death, we should be willing to die.

CALL In 1 Corinthians 12, St. Paul uses the human body as a metaphor for the church as the body of Christ, pointing out that each person is like an eye or an ear, a hand or a foot. All the parts are needed for the body to function at full capacity, and no one person can be all of those parts. Finite beings that we are, we cannot be all things to all people and we cannot as individuals duplicate the work of Christ. We must "specialize" in our ministry, be focused in our call. Our specialty is related to our vision of the work that Christ calls us to do in the world and what he wants to achieve through us. Our spiritual formation should give us such a vision.

Some supposed hallmarks of a solid spirituality actually are more the product of a specific time or culture. For example, unquestioning obedience to one's spiritual superiors was heavily stressed in pre–Vatican II Roman Catholicism, just as unquestioning loyalty to papal declarations is still stressed today. St. Paul said that women should be silent in church, a dictum that today is widely thought to be inapplicable. Some will see rapid congregational growth as a sign of God's favor and of their own spiritual prowess, but numerical growth does not of itself signify the presence of Christ; more important is why the growth is taking place and whether people truly are being led into a deeper relationship with God.

But God asks us to be faithful to whatever call we have been given, whatever our success in the eyes of the world or our denominational colleagues. And the characteristics of sound spirituality listed above cut across time and denominational lines. They hold true for any ministry in any culture. And so an important question that all clergy must ask themselves is, Am I being faithful, and if so, to whom or to what?

We have reviewed some of the signs of a sound spirituality. But knowledge of these on its own does not show us what comprises a healthy spirituality or how to achieve it. To this topic we now turn our attention.

2

SPIRITUALITY IN GENERAL

HAT IS A SPIRITUALITY? In one sense, my spirituality is how I relate to God. My spirituality may be good or bad because I can have either a good relationship with God through Christ or a bad one through preferring my own will to God's. Even Satan has a relationship to God, although it is one of hatred rather than love.

Ronald Rolheiser, in his book *The Holy Longing*, defines our spirituality as the way in which we direct the passion within us. Rolheiser notes that God created each human being with an intense fire within that must find expression. We can interpret this in terms of what Augustine means when he says our hearts were made for God and cannot rest until they rest in God. But restless hearts must put their energy somewhere. Where we put that energy defines our spirituality.

Using spirituality in Rolheiser's broad sense, some people can dissipate their spirituality by seeking too many things. Others can seek only one or two things, thereby focusing their energy in a limited number of directions, but still be seeking things that cannot bring rest to their hearts. Then there are those who seek the one thing worth seeking: God. These are the saints whose desire for God is single-minded.

These two definitions of spirituality—our relation to God and where we direct our inner fire—useful as they may be, are not precise enough for an individual to define his or her own personal spirituality. To say that my relationship with God is good or bad is to say little of practical value because it provides no specifics about how I might improve or make decisions about my ministry. To say that I focus my energies primarily on God is equally nebulous.

The definition of spirituality that I use is this: *Spirituality is that aspect of my faith that serves to guide me in how I conduct my life. It is the framework within which I operate in my desire to be faithful to God.*

As we saw in chapter 1, none of us, including clergy, can or should attempt to duplicate the work of Christ in all its aspects, nor do any of us possess the divine-human nature that he has. Jesus Christ is unique in history, but his work continues through his church. The members of the church are members of Christ's extended body, and Christ charged them with carrying on his work in the world. St. Paul, in 1 Corinthians 12, says how important it is for each member of the body to carry out the function that God assigned to it. He notes pointedly that it is a mistake for any member of Christ's body with one God-appointed function to assume instead the work of a different member. The parts must function together in their proper roles for the body to be healthy. Your appropriation of the work of another member means not only that your own role will go unfilled, but also that you may be depriving someone else of the opportunity for ministry.

Similarly, we cannot live all of the truths of our faith and carry out all of the ministries of Christ. According to the nature of the church and Christ's own intention, it is the church, the entire body of Christ, that is to carry on the work of Christ, not one individual member.

~ 15 ~

Thus, each person focuses on one or a few aspects of our faith and Christ's work that are especially attractive to him or her. One person may be attracted to Christ the teacher, another to Christ the healer, and yet another to Christ's compassion for the poor and the oppressed. Or one person may be attracted to the wonder of the transfiguration, another to the passion, and yet another to the humble fidelity of Mary, Christ's mother.

OUR CALL AS CHRISTIANS

Few people can be specialists in more than two or three disciplines. So much knowledge is available today that even experts in a field generally must specialize if they wish to stay abreast of advances. God is not merely vast; God is infinite. The mysteries of our faith, by definition, surpass the natural capabilities of our intellects. Yet we are called by Christ and through Christ to share in the knowledge of God.

We can expand our knowledge about God—that is, theology—almost indefinitely. We can study the Scriptures and the writings of the great theologians through the ages. We can talk about theology with others versed in the field and teach theology to our congregations. But theology is an intellectual pursuit. We ought not to be puffed up if we are learned in theology, because Satan knows more theology than all human theologians put together.

Ultimately, the knowledge of God cannot be communicated in words, nor can it be taught. It does not come from seminary professors, brilliant sermons, or skilled teaching. It comes only from God. Because we are created beings and God is uncreated, because we are finite and God is infinite, because we are limited to the plane of creation and God is transcendent, only God can lift us, by sheer grace, into God's own divine life. There we can come to know God as God is.

Why would God do such a thing? Certainly, there is no compulsion on God's part to grant such a generous gift. But the fire within that Rolheiser describes and the longing that Augustine talks about were placed in us by God as part of our human nature. We yearn to know God, and we cannot truly be at peace until we *do* know God.

OUR NEED FOR THE INCARNATION

How could even God bridge the infinite gap between Godself and us? The answer to this question is found in the glorious mystery of love called the incarnation. Through Jesus Christ, who is one person with two natures, divine and human, the gap has been closed.

Although through Jesus Christ it is possible for us to be drawn into union with God in love, God still requires our consent to allow this union to grow to maturity. First, as clergy and as Christians, we must accept the invitation to come into union with God by uniting ourselves to Christ's body, the church, and we must open ourselves to God's transforming grace, which alone can bring us to spiritual maturity, which is a more complete sharing in the life of God through Christ. It is in this way that we can come to know God rather than merely to know about God. It is in this way that we are brought to perfection by becoming present to God in the wholeness of our being.

Thus, our spirituality is the foundation on which we build our continuing acceptance of God's invitation to union and our opening of ourselves to the work that only God can do within us. It is the framework for the house that God will build in which God and we will dwell together, bound in love.

The importance of keeping the goal before us as we engage in ministry cannot be overemphasized, for the goal for ourselves and for those to whom we minister is nothing less than

God. God is what our hearts instinctively long for. God is the objective that we should be willing to give up all else to achieve. God is the only being who can, as Rolheiser notes, satisfy our holy longing.

OUR NEED TO KNOW WHAT IS IMPORTANT

A minister friend of mine told me that he was quite hurt and upset when a parishioner told him after a Sunday service that she was deeply disappointed in him. Many other parishioners had told him how much they had enjoyed the service and how fine a sermon he had preached, but what he focused on was the negative comment of this one parishioner.

What was it that had distressed the parishioner? Was it a failure to visit her in the hospital? A lack of compassion for a recent death in her family? Some terrible blunder he had made during the service? No, it was none of these. The problem was that the minister had not noted during the announcement time a meeting that the parishioner thought he should have mentioned. The meeting was not even a meeting at that church, nor had the parishioner herself volunteered to make the announcement when the minister failed to do it. But the parishioner's deep disappointment over what she saw as a blatant error ruined his day.

The unhappy parishioner contacted other parishioners with her complaint. Fortunately, one of the parish leaders heard about it and called the minister. His advice to the minister was simple. "We hired you to preach and to conduct the worship service, not to make announcements. Forget about what she is saying."

This led the minister to reflect on his role in the church. He was called to preach God's word and to conduct the Sunday worship. He was called to teach and to visit the sick. But no, he had not been called there to make announcements.

This was an important lesson for this loving and experienced minister to learn, and he learned it from one of his parishioners. Concentrate on what is important. Concentrate on doing what you as the minister are supposed to do as pastor of the flock. Don't worry about the minutiae that others should be taking care of. And don't be upset by criticism for not doing what you are not responsible for.

Any minister must set priorities and hold to them. It is easy to get sidetracked by parishioners who want you to make announcements. And many ministers are easily sidetracked into "making announcements" ministries because they do not have a clear vision of what is important and it is easier to go with the flow than to struggle to come up with a vision and live according to it. It is easier to live according to the expectations of the vocal parishioners than it is to be a living example of a Christ-ordered life.

Priorities, deciding what is most important and what can safely be ignored, fall out almost automatically from a well-thought-out spirituality. Providing a framework within which a minister can determine what he or she should be doing and why is one of the basic benefits of a spirituality. A spirituality helps concentrate the "fire within," the passion in every human heart, so that it is not scattered and dissipated.

THE LIFE EFFECTS OF A SPIRITUALITY

We will explore the process of finding a spirituality in the second section of this book, but before giving specific examples of spiritualities, we look at the effects that a spirituality will have on how we live.

According to Rolheiser's definition of a spirituality—how we direct the passion within us—a spirituality does not have to be oriented toward God. There are secular spiritualities and even immoral or evil spiritualities.

Suppose, for example, that Jim has the acquisition of money as his spirituality. Then Jim will direct his energy, his time, and his action toward acquiring money. If Jim is single-minded in his pursuit of money, then an action will be judged as good or bad based on whether or not it is likely to help Jim acquire more money. If Jim takes an action that will destroy someone's reputation or livelihood, the effect on that person will be of little or no concern to Jim as long as the action garners him a profit. Jim's priority is clear: accumulate ever greater wealth.

Suppose we look at Jim's life from the viewpoint of prayer, study, and ministry. Jim is not engaged in Christian ministry, nor does he pray in the usual Christian sense, but aspects of his life are analogs of prayer, study, and ministry.

Prayer in a Christian sense is directing heart, mind, and action toward the love and glory of God. That is, prayer is orienting ourselves toward our highest priority as Christians. Jim's highest priority is money, so his "prayer" consists of directing his heart, mind, and action toward money. Even if we consider prayer in the narrow sense of communicating with God, money is Jim's god. When his communications center on money, he is praying to his god.

When Jim studies, he does not study the Bible, but the *Wall Street Journal* or other books or periodicals that will help him make money. His actions, his "ministry" to his god, consist of taking steps to make more money.

I have painted Jim as an extreme case. Few people are so unswervingly oriented toward a secular goal. But those who are so oriented are likely to achieve it. Your spirituality is where your passion and energy are directed, and if your passion and energy are focused on one particular objective, you may well succeed in achieving that objective.

Let's now look at an example of a Christian spirituality.

Jane is a medical doctor and a committed Christian. She wants to use her training and skill in the service of healing. She always holds Jesus in her mind as a man of immense compassion who cared deeply about those who suffer and who used his own power to heal many sick people. Her spirituality, her passion, is healing.

At the beginning of every day Jane lifts her patients up to God, praying in a special way for those who are the most critically ill. She also asks God to give peace to the families of those patients. She views her medical practice as her Christian ministry and asks God to let her patients see the love that Christ has for them through the care and compassion she tries to give to her patients. Her study includes not only meditating on the great healing miracles of Jesus, but also staying current with the latest developments in her specialty so that she can give the best and most up-to-date care.

Neither Jim nor Jane is an ordained clergyperson, but each has a spirituality. Jim's is a secular spirituality. Jane's could be a secular spirituality because she could strive to be an excellent doctor without being a Christian, but she has made her passion for medicine into a Christian spirituality by her devotion to Jesus and by perceiving her work as his work. It is likely that her Christian spirituality makes her more compassionate and attentive to her patients as human beings and also inspires her to add the powerful component of Christian prayer to her medical practice.

Because no one, not even ministers, can reflect all aspects of Christ's own spirituality, which was a universal spirituality, ministers, like Jane and all Christians, must narrow their spiritual focus according to that aspect of their faith or work which most attracts their inner passion.

Having talked about spirituality in general, we move on to discuss clergy spirituality.

3

SPIRITUALITY AND CLERGY

HAT'S SPECIAL ABOUT CLERGY? In chapter 2 we explored spirituality in general. Now we investigate aspects of spirituality that apply more particularly to the clergy. In order to set the stage for this discussion, we must ask ourselves what distinguishes the clergy from the laity.

Some aspects of clergy life have little impact on spirituality. The fact that clergy, most often, have graduated from a seminary, for example, in and of itself has minimal spiritual impact. But the fact that clergy are seen by their congregations as theologically knowledgeable can make a difference in how clergy spirituality is perceived by themselves and by others. Here we look at five attributes of clergy that can, and probably should, affect clergy spirituality.

First, clergy are called to their vocation by God. Traditionally, when seeking to enter the ordained ministry, a person does so in the belief that God has given him or her an indication that that is what God wills.

Second, clergy are expected to be teachers, counselors, and guides. The laity look to the clergy for spiritual and moral guidance and for sound teaching. Although the laity do not always follow the clergy's advice, they do expect their clergy to ground their advice and teaching in Scripture and orthodox theology. When the laity have questions about Scripture, morals, or theology, they usually ask the clergy for answers. Clergy, of course, are expected to keep the confidences of those who come to them in private for guidance, and this too can have spiritual implications because it tends to isolate clergy and drive them in on themselves.

Third, clergy are visible symbols of Christ and his church. Whether the clergy like it or not, they are viewed in this special way by their communities. The church, or at least their own church, is often judged by their lives, words, and actions. They are on public display much more so than the members of their congregations. If a parishioner engages in immoral conduct, the congregation and its public image are much less affected than if its pastor is discovered to have engaged in immoral conduct. Just as the clergy hold up Christ as an example of how to live a Christian life, they themselves are expected to be models for a Christian life. They are supposed to exhibit "Christlike" virtues such as compassion, mercy, and love so that others can see these virtues reflected in the clergyperson's life. If the parishioners see a lack of these virtues in their pastor, they will lose confidence in him or her as a spiritual leader, especially in this age in which respect for the clergy must be earned rather than assumed to come with the office.

Fourth, clergy are expected to intercede with God for their people. Most congregants consider clergy to be intermediaries between God and themselves, even in those instances in which members are assumed to have a personal relationship with God. The role of intermediary is particularly pronounced in denominations that have a sacramental priesthood, such as, for example, Roman Catholicism.

Fifth, clergy are expected to be men and women of prayer.

In one sense, this observation is merely a repetition on the immediately preceding one. But it includes the expectation that clergy will lead their congregations in prayer. They are the prayer and worship leaders. Most often, they plan the worship of their church and set its tone.

All these responsibilities can be heavy burdens for clergy to bear. Pastor Jones from chapter 1 was being ground down by such expectations. She was required to be a resource to her flock, but she did not feel free to let her flock be a resource to her, nor could she freely discuss with others the confidences of those who sought her support. She could not say to a hurting counselee, "I am too tired and troubled myself to see you today. Find someone else to help you." Just as Jesus found it hard to get time to be alone because of the multitudes that came to him for healing and teaching, a clergyperson often is unable to get time to be alone, even when he or she needs it most. All too frequently, clergy lives are comprised of work that is not balanced by rest and play.

We now turn to some of the implications of personal spirituality for the special aspects of being a member of the clergy.

CLERGY AS SYMBOLS AND AS TEACHERS

We live in a society characterized by egocentrism. Research done by respected figures such as George Barna and Robert Wuthnow indicates that the vast majority of the population of the United States believes in God. That is the good news. The bad news is that many "believers" pick and choose what God they believe in. Denominations and creeds quite often are considered to be relics of the past, straitjackets on the development of an "authentic" personal spirituality.

The emphasis on what "I believe," as opposed to what the church believes, leads not to many "orthodoxies" but away from any orthodoxy whatsoever. Some writers have argued that heresy cannot exist today because each person is free to interpret Scripture as he or she pleases and can listen for what God has to say independently of any outside authority that might set constraints on what theological conclusions are admissible. A Christian might not even have any articles of faith that warrant being called theological, because eclectic individualism, carried to its extreme, is based solely on an emotional relationship with an ill-defined and nebulous entity called "God."

In no way am I trying to minimize the importance of either salvation or human emotions, but I do suggest that spirituality, especially for clergy, cannot be grounded in the emotions. Spirituality requires intellectual content because it must form the basis for practical decisions. A spirituality founded solely on sentiment, devoid of intellectual content, risks being little more than "If it feels good, do it." Prayer may degenerate into "emotional masturbation," and worship may be valued more for its capacity to entertain than to provide an encounter with the living God.

Spirituality implies faith, but faith in a deeper sense than just believing that God will make everything turn out all right or that eventually we will all get our "eternal reward." We all, clergy included, experience times when we feel as if God is "asleep in the back of the boat." But even in those times, we trust in God. And if we have trust in God, then we trust also in what God has revealed through Christ and the church, indeed, what God has revealed to humanity down through the ages from the Old Testament through the New.

The ultimate revelation of God is in and through our Lord Jesus Christ. Jesus is more than a symbol of God's mercy, more than a ticket to heaven. Jesus is the way, the truth, and the life (John 14:6). What we believe about Jesus and how we interpret that belief in our lives is, in essence, our spirituality.

The question "Who do you say that I am?" is as relevant today as it was when Jesus first asked it of his disciples.

According to the ancient creeds and statements by and about Christ in the Scriptures, Jesus is both human and divine, one person with two natures, God and human being. If this were not so, he could not save us. He could not bridge the infinite gap that exists between God and creation. If he were only a human being, his sacrifice on the cross would have no more value than the death of any human martyr for a cause. If he were only God, he could not be said to be truly one of us. He could not offer himself as a second Adam because he would not be of the same nature as Adam.

A sound spirituality must first and foremost recognize that Jesus Christ is a real human being, born of a woman, and that he also is the eternal Son of God, the Father. Our spirituality must be founded on the rock that is Christ, not on anything less, if it is to be a Christian spirituality.

Lacking any theological foundation for their faith and sensing that emotions alone are not adequate for a deep relationship with God, many Christians revert to moralism, an emphasis on the Ten Commandments or other rules for living according to God's law. Ironically, such an attitude is more suited to the Old Testament and the emphasis on strict compliance with the Mosaic law than it is to the New Testament, in which Jesus made it clear that the spirit of the law and our internal dispositions are what matter most.

I might sum up what I have been trying to say as follows: Sound spirituality must be founded on sound theology, the core of which is belief in Jesus Christ as the son of Mary and the Son of God. If clergy are not clear in their own minds about who Jesus is, they cannot convey clarity to others. If the spirituality of clergy is based on emotions, it will collapse as soon as the emotionalism withers. It requires that the clergy take a stand on what one must believe in order to be a Christian and base their own spirituality on those beliefs. When Peter answered Jesus' fundamental question by boldly stating, "You are the Christ, the Son of the living God," Jesus did not respond, "Good, Peter, if that's the way you feel. How do the rest of you feel about that?" Jesus called Peter "blessed" because Peter's confession stemmed not from human thought but from a revelation of God (Matthew 16:17).

The spirituality of a clergyperson must be a window through which the congregation can see Jesus. The spiritualty of a clergyperson must convey light and faith in a dark and uncertain age. As visible signs of the church, clergy must symbolize the way, the truth, and the life that is Christ. As teachers, they must have something of substance to teach. If the clergy fall victim to relativism and sentimentality, they may still be signs, but they will no longer be signs of Christ and his church. They may still have something to teach, but it will not be Christianity.

CLERGY AS INTERMEDIARIES
AND AS LEADERS

In an era of individualistic religious faith, many people are less likely to feel any need for intermediaries between themselves and God. Even those who are esteemed as being spiritually advanced, such as gurus and "enlightened ones," are seen more as teachers who help others achieve their own exalted state than as intercessors with a transcendent God.

The so-called New Age is primarily a revival of ancient Gnostic ideas combined with a strong dose of Pelagianism. Right knowledge combined with right spiritual practices allows a human being to gain access to the divine, if not, in fact, to become divine. There is no need for Christ as savior or the Holy Spirit as sanctifier because religion becomes a "do-it-yourself job." In such a context, it is not entirely clear what prayer means or why communal worship is important.

And yet the goal of both Christians and New Age advocates is the same: to grow into the life of God. It is the means that are radically different, even if we assume that God is God for everyone. New Age devotees, together with an increasing number of people who claim to be Christian, believe that their own efforts will bring about union with, or transformation into, God. Orthodox Christians believe that it is only through Christ, by the power of the Holy Spirit, that we are able to share in the life of God and thereby come to know God as God knows us. If we are able to bootstrap our way into "salvation," whatever salvation means, then we have no need for anyone but ourselves—no need for Christ, much less for clergy.

Therefore the clergy as spiritual leaders must live and teach a spirituality that demonstrates our utter dependence on God's free gift of grace if we are to achieve the destiny to which God calls us. Clergy spirituality has a special obligation to proclaim Jesus Christ, the Son of God the Father, as the way, the truth, and the life. Clergy spirituality also must proclaim the sanctifying power of the Holy Spirit, for another aspect of creedal Christianity that is in decline is belief in the Trinity. Despite the difficulties surrounding this mystery of faith, the Trinity is essential to a right understanding of Christ and his saving work.

Clergy as leaders of worship and prayer must have a clear vision of what prayer is and the goals of worship. Clergy should be seen as persons who pray always, not in the narrower sense of speaking to God, but in the sense of directing their entire lives to the love and service of God. We are told by Scripture to pray always (1 Thessalonians 5:17). We are told that whatever we do ought to be done for the glory of God

(1 Corinthians 10:31). Clergy, through their spirituality, are to live a life of prayer and a life that is a prayer.

But why do clergy, or why does any Christian, pray and worship? Prayer and worship are for our sake, not for God's. Prayer and worship are means by which we can say a continual yes to God's invitation to come in love and open ourselves to transforming grace. As Martin Smith states in *The Word Is Very Near You*, "Our prayer is not making conversation with God. It is joining the conversation that is already going on in God."

Worship is an opportunity to place ourselves on the altar as an offering in union with Christ to the Father for our lives and for the life of the world. What, indeed, are the goals of the worship for which clergy are responsible?

WHY DO WE WORSHIP?

If clergy are to be most effective as leaders in worship, they must have a clear vision of why they are worshiping. This means that they must put aside their own desires and ask themselves what God wants to achieve through communal worship. All worship leaders are tempted to make themselves the center of attention. Many of us find our voices to be so attractive and our message so irresistible that we forget that we are instruments of God. If God cannot act through us because we get in God's way by our pride or self-importance, we are failing in the vocation to which God called us.

Worship leaders must always keep in mind that worship is God's gift to us. We need our communal worship; God doesn't need it. God will be God without our worship, but we will be less open to God and fail to take advantage of a powerful spiritual aid if we neglect communal worship. Here are four reasons why worship is vitally important for Christian growth.

First, worship should open us to God's transforming grace.

We should come to worship expecting to relate to God and Christ in intimacy and love, and we should leave worship strengthened to carry on Christ's work in the world. In the worship service we are exposed to God's word and should open our hearts and minds to allow that word to act within us. We may also receive ordinances or sacraments as a special means of grace.

Second, worship should make us realize that we share in the priesthood of Christ and that we exercise that priesthood in our worship. Worship is not the work of the clergy but all of the people of God assembled. We might even say that in communal worship we are joined with the entire church in all times and places because we recognize our communion with all members of the body of Christ. Worship should help us to see that we need the body of Christ and the body of Christ needs us because we all share in the ministry of Christ and we all have roles to play in completing that ministry.

Third, worship should make us aware of God's presence in the mysteries that we celebrate together. We should recognize that we are brought into contact with the mystery of God and the saving work of Christ in the public worship of the church and in the ordinances and sacraments, most particularly the Lord's Supper. Worship, even in nonliturgical churches, should be seen as a mystery play in which we come into intimate contact with the mysteries that we celebrate.

Fourth, worship has a teaching function in which we are reminded of, and deepen our understanding of, the truths of our faith and their application to our lives. In fact, the Sunday service often is the only opportunity to provide any instruction in the faith to many members of the congregation. The teaching in worship should go beyond platitudes or advice on leading a moral life. It should make members aware that the goal of their Christian calling is to be drawn by God into the life of God through Christ so that they can come to know God. It should remind them that through God's love dwelling in them, they are to do Christ's work of transforming the world. The teaching should inspire parishioners not only to lead a righteous life but also to live a holy life.

CAN SPIRITUALITY COVER ALL BASES?

In this chapter we have looked at the special roles that clergy play in the church and how their spiritualities must be integrated with those roles if the clergy are to carry out their function as the denominationally ordained spiritual leaders for the people of God. Is it possible for any one person to have a spirituality that attempts to do so much? Almost certainly, the answer is no. Some clergy will focus primarily on worship, others on teaching, others on pastoral counseling, and so on. Clergy cannot be all things to all people, although some die trying. That death may be spiritual, physical, or mental.

But clergy, because they are recognized spiritual leaders, generally must have a spirituality that relates to the forms of leadership that they believe to be their strengths, or the forms of leadership to which they believe God has called them, even if they recognize that they are weak in some areas. This requires that they take into account the special considerations advanced in this chapter when they choose a spirituality. In the meantime, clergy must recognize that although they are more visible representatives of Christ than are most laity, their spiritualities will still be personal and focused. I will have more to say about choosing a spirituality in the second part of this book.

4

A PERSONAL SPIRITUALITY
FOR CLERGY

OWARD A PASTORAL SPIRITUALITY
Thus far we have considered spirituality in general and spirituality as applied to clergy. Now we want to consider spirituality as applied to an individual member of the clergy.

Some aspects of spirituality apply to all Christians. Every Christian has special gifts, interests, talents, and so forth that can be brought to his or her unique pilgrimage. Each Christian's spirituality should somehow be related to and express those special attributes. The same is true, of course, for clergy, but clergy have special responsibilities within the church. They have received a call from God to be leaders of God's people; consequently, a pastor's spirituality must somehow encompass and express that call. Even though the laity are also called to share in the ministry of Christ, they are not called to do so as publicly as the clergy. They do not represent the church to the same extent that the clergy do. That is, the clergy, by virtue of their office and leadership roles, generally are more visible symbols of Christ than laypersons.

A pastor's spirituality will be not only his or her personal spirituality, but also the framework within which he or she carries out pastoral functions. It will be a source of direction for his or her ministry, a beacon to guide decisions, and a source of consolation in times of trouble. It will serve like the rudder that keeps the ship on course, even in stormy seas. It will be a pastoral spirituality.

Let us consider again one of the situations portrayed at the beginning of chapter 1.

BROTHER JOHNSON REVISITED

Let's revisit Brother Johnson from the example that began chapter 1. Brother Johnson is wrestling with important life issues that should be addressed within the context not only of his ministry but also of his spirituality. What is his spirituality? None is evident from the meager facts given, but what spiritualities might he have and how would each spirituality help him make his decision?

Suppose Brother Johnson's passion centers on evangelism, bringing the good news to as many people as possible. Each day Brother Johnson prays for the unconverted and that he may receive power from the Holy Spirit to bring people to Christ. He reads books and attends workshops on methods to evangelize and has encouraged his congregation to give programs, such as Alpha, that are directed at attracting the unchurched.

Although Brother Johnson's evangelistic spirituality will not automatically give him the answer to his questions, it does give him a framework within which to seek answers. For example, it is unlikely that he will want to remain passively at his current church until he can retire. His desire to convert souls to Christ will not allow him to do so. If he remains where he is, he will want to direct his attention to the conversion of the newest residents in his church's neighborhood.

But Brother Johnson may recognize that his particular style of preaching and worship is not likely to appeal to the cultures that he now finds in the area of his church. So he may, with a clear conscience, seek a position in which he feels that he could be more effective, or he might ask his denominational judicatory to send a pastor to replace him who would relate well to the new neighbors. It could be an act of humility and sacrifice if Brother Johnson were willing to cede his leadership to someone else who could evangelize the area more effectively than he could.

Suppose Brother Johnson's passion is youth work. If many youth are moving into the area near the church, he might try to develop programs to benefit youth. If there is a problem with latchkey children, he might start an after-school tutoring and play program in the church's fellowship hall. He might seek grants to provide health care for youth who otherwise might not ever see a doctor. In other words, if he finds the opportunity to express his passion for youth in his current situation, Brother Johnson might well stay where he is and find new programs to express that passion. On the other hand, if the neighborhood is aging, he might seek a new situation in which he would be able to reach more young people. Knowing when to say no so that God's yes can occur is part of spiritual maturity.

KNOWING YOURSELF

Because each Christian is unique, each Christian will have a spirituality that is unique. Two Christians may have the same passion, the same aspect of faith that they find especially attractive and by which they are especially motivated, but their spiritualities, while similar, cannot be the same, because they have many differences both as individuals and in the circumstances in which they will live out their spiritualities.

The same, of course, holds true for pastors. Two pastors may both have a passion for evangelism, but they will express this passion in different ways. Their spiritualities will help them form a "pattern of life," which can be a substantial aid to spiritual growth. (We will explore the notion of a pattern of life at length in chapter 6.) But their patterns of life almost certainly will have significant differences because patterns of life are based not only on one's spirituality, but also on other factors such as temperament and work environment.

You may not even be sure yet what your spirituality is. (We will see more about finding your own personal spirituality in chapter 6.) One thing is certain: your spirituality will be yours and no one else's. You are not only unique as a Christian, but also unique as a pastor. Trying to identify your spirituality should help you to know more about yourself, to understand both your call to ministry and your motives for acting as you do.

How do we know if a spirituality is "working"? What are signs that a spirituality, or the manner in which it is being lived out, is not working? We consider these questions now.

5

GOOD FRUITS AND WARNING SIGNS

OTIVES ARE VITAL
In chapter 1 we looked at four signs of a sound spirituality: humility, compassion, love, and a clear vision of what Christ is calling us to do. We could say, therefore, that a spirituality is unhealthy if one or more of these signs is missing. That is, a spirituality that engenders pride, judgmentalism, legalism, indifference toward others, and dissipation of our spiritual energy needs some serious midcourse correction to get back on track with Christ's vision.

As a rule, however, the matter is much more subtle than this. Signs of an unhealthy spirituality are usually not so blatant as a hateful pastor or a minister who always wants to be the center of attention. The signs of a diseased spirituality can easily be missed not only by the clergy themselves but also by their congregations. All may appear to be going quite well. The congregation is growing in numbers. The sermons are well received. The Sunday school classes are filled. But something may be missing in the spiritual life of the pastor that can negatively impact both the pastor and the congregation. Here we will try to identify some of the warning signs to look for when a spirituality is not what it should be.

First, recall the definition of spirituality that we are using: *Spirituality is that aspect of my faith that serves to guide me in how I conduct my life. It is the framework within which I operate in my desire to be faithful to God.*

As noted earlier, Ronald Rolheiser defines spirituality as the way in which we direct our inner passion. By this definition, spirituality need not even be related to religion, since a person's passion may be directed to worldly interests such as money, or scattered over many different areas. Just as someone can direct his or her passion in ways that lead away from God, so too spirituality, in the sense that we are using the concept, can be false. It can have the appearance of a desire to please God while in reality being motivated primarily by other concerns, such as being well thought of or striving for a position of power within a denomination.

To paraphrase a line from T. S. Eliot's play *Murder in the Cathedral,* "This is the greatest temptation of all: to do the right thing for the wrong reason." I may have as my spirituality the preparation of members of the body of Christ for evangelism. I could, in fact, build my prayer, study, and actions around this theme. I might even be quite successful in sending missionaries out from my congregation to start other local congregations or even into the foreign mission field. I might even acquire an impressive reputation for my work and be invited to speak at national conferences or to be on the team for major revivals.

But Jesus looks at the heart, not the outward appearances. The question that Jesus asks is not what am I doing, but why am I doing what I am doing. If I am training evangelists to enhance my own reputation, then I have lost sight of the purpose of any spirituality, which is to accept God's invitation to come in love and open myself to transforming grace. I may become so wrapped up in my preparation of evangelists that I begin to think that I am the one responsible for my success and become angry when people fail to compliment me on it. I may see myself in competition with others with the same ministry and try to find opportunities to aggrandize myself and to belittle them; I may also get angry when one of them is honored and I am not. If so, then although the work that I am engaged in is good, my spirituality is poisoned by improper motives. And the improper motives begin to reveal their presence in pride and a lack of charity. Instead of being consumed with passion for the glory of God and the salvation of souls, I am consumed with desire for personal recognition. I want to be successful so that I will be seen to be successful by those whose respect I treasure. The distorted motivation may be hard to finger but may reveal itself in undue depression and overcommitment to work.

Unfortunately, we are all fallen beings, so too often we are pulled toward egotism and pride. Even when we start out with good intentions, our motives may become warped by the praise we receive or by the money we earn on the lecture circuit. What should we look at for signs that our spirituality is being corrupted, not in terms of the focus of our ministry but in terms of why we behave as we do?

WARNING SIGNS

PRIDE In its worst form, pride is making ourselves our own god. We ourselves become the measure of what is right and wrong, desirable and undesirable. We are confident that we have power of ourselves to bring about splendid results. We might secretly feel that God is lucky to have us on the team, since clearly God would be worse off without our efforts.

But ministers rarely make themselves their own god. Most clergy at least acknowledge the notion that they cannot even say "Jesus is Lord" except by the grace of the Holy Spirit.

Most also will admit that they are only the instruments of God, servants of Christ, and unworthy servants at that.

Pride is most likely to manifest itself in the desire to control. Clergy can describe themselves as "servants of the servants of God," but, as the old quip goes, sometimes the church suffers from a servant problem.

Clergy are expected to lead, but that leadership should be servant leadership. The model for servant leadership is, of course, Jesus. Although he was God and could have demanded complete and unquestioning obedience from his disciples by an authority greater than that of any clergy, he gently taught his disciples, encouraged them, empowered them for their own ministries, and, ultimately, turned his work in the world over to them.

When a minister always expects others to do things his way, rather than teaching and encouraging others to develop and use their own unique skills and talents, that minister is asserting that his way is God's way. In effect, he is binding the Spirit by implying that God cannot work through others in any way but the minister's way. The minister risks mistaking his own will for God's. This is pride, but pride that easily masquerades as faithfulness. "Follow me," the minister says, "and you are following God." Thus, the minister is replacing God in his own eyes and the eyes of his flock.

The role of a wise minister, like that of a wise parent, is to help her children grow to spiritual maturity, not to control them and keep them forever dependent on the parent. Clergy spirituality must be based on this principle in order to be healthy and to bring spiritual health to the congregation.

LEGALISM It is easier to be "faithful" in a religion of rules than in a religion of love. If we belong to an organization in which there is a clearly defined set of expectations about what members should and should not do, we can use a check sheet to determine whether or not we are fulfilling our membership obligations. Why we do something is not as important as that we do it. We may hate other members and secretly pray for God to punish them, but as long as we give them the proper greeting required by the organization, we can remain in good standing.

A warning sign that clergy spirituality might not be all it should be is an inordinate attention to rules. This is not to suggest that clergy, as part of their responsibilities of leadership, should refrain from teaching sound moral principles or rebuking a member who is engaged in openly scandalous behavior. Jesus did not condone sin, but neither did he condemn the sinner. He told sinners to go and sin no more, to desist from their sinful behavior lest eventually it destroy them.

The ones whom Jesus got angry with were those who thought of themselves as righteous because they kept the strictures of the Mosaic law and who thought that their adherence to the rules set them above other men and women, particularly sinners. But, as Jesus pointed out to them, their blind obedience to the law often contradicted not only love of their neighbors but also love of God. Jesus, in love, healed the sick on the Sabbath, and the Pharisees got angry. Jesus' disciples picked grain on the Sabbath because they were hungry, and the Pharisees got angry. The Pharisees made a public show of their obedience to the law, and Jesus got angry.

Again and again Jesus stressed that what was in the heart, the motives for actions, counted more than the actions themselves. Jesus breathed life and power into the will of God, while the legalists demanded adherence to a standard that not only was impossible to keep faithfully but also resulted in spiritual stagnation instead of spiritual growth.

One form that legalism takes is scrupulosity in which

someone worries excessively about whether he or she is doing things exactly as God wants them done. The scrupulous individual is so anxious about what to do as to lose all sense of perspective. The least defect in some action, such as a mistake in a sermon, may be viewed as a grave offense against God. Scrupulosity as a psychological ailment may require professional treatment. But scrupulosity also may indicate a lapse into legalism, where the actions become more important in themselves and in how they are carried out than the motives behind them. Moreover, the scrupulous person often is more afraid of God as a stern judge than in love with a God who desires intimate union with that person through Christ. Sometimes, scrupulosity disguises itself as an excessive attention to traditions without reference to the rationales that underlie them.

While legalism can be quite damaging to the individual clergyperson, it can be even more damaging to his or her congregation. A legalistic clergyperson will generally emphasize rules by which parishioners are to live, sometimes backed by threats of discipline, expulsion, or even hell if they do not obey the rules. Often, the Ten Commandments become the focus of attention rather than the good news of God among us. The clergyperson often assumes the role of being arbiter of who is in a state of grace and who is not and personally decides the penance that must be performed before an errant sheep will be allowed back into the fold.

Again, I am not suggesting that clergy should not have standards or that there are no circumstances in which a parishioner should be excluded from communion. The words of Jesus himself establish a process for dealing with errant brothers and sisters (Matthew 18:15-17), but when the minister assumes the role of Christ as lawgiver instead of Christ the good shepherd, there is spiritual danger for both the clergy and sinners alike. Actually, Christ gave us only one new commandment: to love others as we have first been loved. And he gave us a new way of looking at the old commandments: to live by their spirit and not by their letter. We are called to be brothers and sisters of Jesus, not slaves under the law. Where legalism is emphasized, often there is more fear and judgmentalism than love. It is difficult, in fact impossible, to be afraid of God and deeply in love with him at the same time. Fear is not the same thing as respect, reverence, or awe. The closer we are to God in love, the greater we are in awe of God.

APATHY As clergy become burned out, they usually become more apathetic to what happens both to themselves and to their congregations. Burned-out clergy are vulnerable to many temptations. Some may rationalize that a sexual affair will restore excitement to their lives. Others may find consolation in alcohol or drugs. Most will find it increasingly difficult to attend to the needs of their parishioners. Some suffer from physical and mental symptoms such as headaches, hypertension, forgetfulness, or tardiness.

A clergyperson's spirituality should sustain her through good times and bad. The spirituality must be a constant reminder of having said yes to the invitation to come into union with God and to serve in the role of a spiritual leader of the people of God. The spirituality must continually open the clergyperson to God's action in and through her to transform both her and her parishioners. This is heavy baggage for both the spirituality and the minister to bear. They cannot bear it alone. The spirituality must be sustained and inspired by the power of the Holy Spirit and by right motives on the part of the minister. The minister must be sustained by God in the role to which God has called her.

If the load seems unbearable, the minister might do well to take a guided retreat of at least eight to ten days to reexamine his spirituality and seek renewal through reconnecting with the only Source of strength that can sustain a minister. (I will have more to say about retreats in the next section, "The Road to a Sound Spirituality.")

A minister must keep in mind that just as God expects her to support others in their times of trial, so too God expects the minister to care for her own needs. Constant self-sacrifice, as seems to be the case with Pastor Jones in chapter 1, can erode the ability of a pastor to minister to others. For example, giving up sleep to spend more time on programs may subvert the health of the minister and detract from the effectiveness of the programs themselves because the minister cannot function at peak performance.

The minister's spirituality also should bring greater focus to his work. It bears repeating that no one, even the most dedicated pastor, can be all things to all people or have expertise, or even significant skill, in every area of the work of the church. If a minister's passion is working with youth, that same minister may have little aptitude for working with the elderly or selecting the music for worship. If the minister's passion, his spirituality, is not a good fit for the church being served, he might consider moving, without feeling guilty, to a situation where his spirituality and the job description are a better match.

In the same vein, a minister should make the people of the congregation aware of her spirituality both prior to a call and afterwards so that they will understand, and hopefully respect, that spirituality. Likewise, the minister should help parishioners to explore their own spiritualities so that they can, and will, carry out those portions of the church's work that they should not reasonably expect the minister to handle.

SECULARIZATION   Ministers who are highly praised by their congregations or a broader public for their work might begin to focus on their success in the eyes of the world and begin to lose sight of whose work they are engaged in. Laudatory articles in the press, a book that receives critical acclaim, or civic awards can be seductive. Ministers who do not have a solid spirituality to keep them on track may lose focus and give undue attention to those projects that have garnered praise rather than focusing on projects in keeping with their spirituality. Ministers can often judge their "attachments" by how agitated they become when their efforts are thwarted.

Success in terms of numbers or other measurable results can be an indication, of course, that God wants a minister to concentrate on the efforts that brought that success. But a minister must always remember that even if the success is real in terms of building the kingdom of God, as opposed to merely racking up numbers, he or she is still the instrument of God. God can and does use flawed instruments in spreading the gospel in powerful ways, St. Paul being a prime example. The minister is a member of the body of Christ with a particular function to perform within that body. Ministers who become sidetracked from their God-willed functions into other functions because they are able to garner greater "success" there may well have fallen into a spiritual trap. The trap can be extremely subtle because we all want to do "well," especially for God.

We should not judge success as the world judges success. Jesus on the cross seemingly was one of the greatest failures of all time. A sound spirituality helps keeps us focused on what is really important and on what God expects of us rather than what the world rewards. There is danger for any minister who has begun to pursue secular success instead of faithfulness to God as expressed in his or her spirituality. Secular success and a solid spirituality can coexist, but the emphasis must be on the latter.

A spirituality is intended to be an aid and should not be allowed to become a trap. A spirituality should, with the help of God, bear good fruits. Just as we have examined warning signs of an unhealthy spirituality, so also should we now examine the fruits of a healthy one.

SIGNS OF A SOUND SPIRITUALITY REVISITED

In chapter 1 we looked at four signs of a sound spirituality. We revisit these briefly in light of this chapter's discussion of warning signs.

Humility. Humility is honesty about oneself. If we have a framework of faith in which we operate, we will, if we are open to it, see ourselves realistically within that framework. We will be able to make decisions concerning how we are called to serve God more readily than if we did not have that framework, our spirituality. We will recognize that we are instruments of God doing the work of Christ with the emphasis that our spirituality brings to our lives. We will neither denigrate nor dissipate our talents, but rather, use them with greater effect because of the discipline that our spirituality provides.

Compassion. Compassion is a nonjudgmental concern for all human beings, whatever their condition or status. Our spirituality helps us recognize that every human being has a place in God's scheme and is deserving of respect and Christian love. We have our place and others have theirs, but we all belong to the humanity that Christ came to save, and we are all called to serve in our own unique ways.

Love. According to the New Commandment of Christ, we are to love others as we have first been loved, even to the point of sacrifice. All healthy spirituality must result in a deeper relationship with God, because God can act more effectively in transforming us, shaping us into what God calls us to become. The deeper our relationship with God, the more we evidence God's love in our lives. If a spirituality does not result in love of God and neighbor, it is not a healthy spirituality.

Call. Each person needs a vision of where, how, and in what ways he or she is called to minister as part of the body of Christ. By definition, a sound spirituality sharpens our conception of the life that Jesus is calling us to live in his name.

Quite often, we are poor judges of our own cases. We need others to help us discern whether we are experiencing good fruits or warning signs. Spiritual direction can help us to view ourselves more objectively as well as discern more clearly where God is leading us. (We will learn more about spiritual direction in chapter 10.)

section 2

THE ROAD
TO A SOUND
SPIRITUALITY

IN PART ONE I DEALT WITH CONCEPTS SUCH AS SPIRITUALITY and ministry. Deliberately, I did not provide any methods for identifying a personal spirituality or what to do with such a spirituality once it was identified. This second part of the book is more "hands on." Its purpose is to provide practical techniques and advice that ministers might use in their spiritual walk.

This part begins with a discussion of a "pattern of life" and that pattern's relationship to one's spirituality. It also offers guidance on identifying one's spirituality.

In chapters 7, 8, and 9 I discuss two important forms of prayer: meditation and contemplation. These prayer techniques can be valuable tools in discerning God's action in our lives, formulating an appropriate response, and opening ourselves more and more to God's transforming grace.

In chapter 10 I discuss spiritual direction and how it can help a pastor to grow spiritually. I also discuss some possible objections to spiritual direction and respond to them. Chapter 11 sets out some additional aids to clergy spirituality, while chapter 12 explores some spiritual issues of particular concern to clergy.

6

SPIRITUAL FORMATION

HAT IS SPIRITUAL FORMATION? Clergy, probably more than most others, recognize that their relationship with God is central to their lives. However, what "relationship with God" means varies from minister to minister and denomination to denomination. I will state my own view of what "relationship with God" means so that I can expand on it as I explore the concept of spiritual formation. Specifically, my relationship with God is my membership in the body of Christ and thereby my becoming a "temple of the Holy Spirit." I relate to God through Christ and am sanctified by the Holy Spirit.

This relationship is central to any Christian spirituality. It is the foundation on which any Christian spirituality is built. From this point on, I will restrict my attention exclusively to Christian spiritualities.

Once my relationship with God is established in Christ and given life by the Holy Spirit, I still am not yet where God intends me to be. I am called to be in union with God in love. I am invited to know God as God knows me. Because such knowledge is totally beyond my natural abilities, it can come only as a gift from God. I somehow must be allowed to share in God's life so that I can, in fact, come to know God directly.

Love of God is central because it is through love that we become conformed to God, that is, become by God's gift what God is by nature. If we do not become like God, we cannot know God directly. Jesus, quoting the Scripture, said, "You shall love the Lord your God with all your heart and soul and mind and strength." This is the essence of the law. But this means that we must belong entirely to God in all aspects of our being. Our wills in particular must choose what we believe God wants of us. As Jesus also said, "Those who love me keep my commandments," which is to say, "Those who love me will integrate their own will with my will." Just as Jesus always did the will of his Father, so we too are to always do the will of Christ, and through Christ be drawn ever more deeply into the life of the Father.

Once we have established our relationship with God through Jesus, we are at the beginning of the transformation that God wants to achieve in us. Hopefully, in our incorporation into the body of Christ, we have declared our openness to God, our willingness to let God take control of our lives to fashion us into whatever God wills us to become.

But even given such openness on our part, God will not act in any two individuals in the same way. There is no universal template for holiness of life, nor is there one set of prayer practices that suits each and every person. God will transform each one of us in the manner that is best for the individual. God may not give us the spiritual gifts that we want, but God will always give us the spiritual gifts that we need, both for personal growth into God and to help those entrusted to our care to grow into God.

Our spiritual formation, then, is this: to develop and to practice a pattern of life that will enable us to cooperate as fully as possible with God as God works in and through us to transform both us and the world. Thus, the first part of spiritual formation is to develop a pattern of life, or, as some call it, a rule of life, suited to our own individual temperament and circumstances. The second part of spiritual formation is to practice that pattern of life. For better accountability and evaluation of whether our pattern of life is what it should be, it is best to have a spiritual director or a spiritual direction group. (I will say more about spiritual direction in chapter 10.)

FORMING A PATTERN OF LIFE

Every pattern of life must include elements of prayer, study, and ministry. What these elements are, however, varies from individual to individual. Moreover, the pattern may evolve over time as the individual grows spiritually as well as when his or her life circumstances change.

The pattern of life does not include all aspects of a minister's life. Rather, it is like the bass line of a musical composition against which a musician is free to improvise. It is an orderly constant in the otherwise changing flow of the minister's everyday life.

An element of a pattern of life must be sufficiently well defined in terms of time and content so that a person can easily tell whether the element has been accomplished. There must be clarity about what is to be done and how often or when it is to be done, because an overly vague element either leads to confusion or imposes no obligation at all. "I will say the Lord's Prayer when I feel like doing so" is precise as to what will be done but unclear as to when it will be done. "I will do something nice once a day" is precise as to time but unclear as to content. "I will offer my day to God as soon as I wake up in the morning" is precise as to both time and content. We now consider the basic elements of a pattern of life.

PRAYER The prayer element of the pattern should include a practice of listening to God or simply placing oneself in the presence of God. Normally, we think of prayer as speaking to God, informing God about our feelings and our needs, praising God for God's goodness, expressing sorrow for our sins. But if we are to be open to God's action in our lives, we must be attentive to God. We must listen for the still, small voice of God that will help us discern what God wants of us instead of what we want of God.

There are a variety of techniques that anyone can use to listen for God or, if God does not choose to speak, to be available to God in humble silence and simplicity. We will explore these techniques in the chapters on meditation and contemplation.

Here are two examples of prayer elements that might form part of a pattern of life:

• Sit quietly for ten minutes each morning after asking God to inspire you with anything that God might want you to know.

• Sit quietly for five minutes, immediately after you arrive at your office for the day, gazing at the cross and thinking about what it means for you and for your ministry.

STUDY I have noted already that our transformation into what God wants us to become is not our work, but the work of the Holy Spirit. It may seem somewhat inconsistent, then, to suggest that a pattern of life should include an element of study. Study can only teach us about God. It cannot of itself bring us into the experience of God.

Nevertheless, study is an important part of a pattern of life for at least two reasons. First, through study we can make ourselves more competent in our performance of God's work. A more complete understanding of what a biblical author intended to say, for example, may help us both in preaching and in leading Bible study classes.

Each one of us is an instrument of God in helping Christians to live more fully in the life of God and in bringing the unconverted to Christ. To be more effective instruments, particularly as ministers, we need to know what we are talking about. If someone gives a false argument against Christianity, for example, an informed minister is more likely to have a ready answer.

Second, God can speak to us through the words encountered in study. The Holy Spirit speaks to us far more often through other people, even nonbelievers, than directly. God can even speak to us by inspiring us with thoughts that are unrelated to what we are studying.

Every preacher has had the experience of someone saying, "That sermon spoke to me personally. It told me exactly what I needed to hear at this time in my life." And yet, from the preacher's point of view, the listener heard something other than what was said in the sermon. Nevertheless, instead of feeling angry that the person did not hear what was said, the preacher rejoices and thanks God for speaking to that person, who was open to God's word. Clergy themselves may have a similar experience when studying. God may give them helpful knowledge even though it does not relate to what they are reading or listening to at the time.

Here are three examples of study elements that might form part of a pattern of life:

- Read and reflect on at least two chapters of Scripture every day.
- Finish at least one book on evangelism or congregational development each month.
- Attend at least two overnight workshops on preaching each year.

MINISTRY   Although all of the people of God should be engaged in ministry, clergy are engaged in ministry in a more intentional way. The laity expect them to do ministry; they are professionals in ministry as well as leaders of it.

Presumably, then, clergy should have no trouble in adding some element of ministry to their pattern of life. But why should they single out some element when so much of their day is involved with ministry? This brings us to the basic question: Why have a pattern of life?

The pattern of life is not something done for its own sake. We do not form a pattern of life just to be able to say that we have one. We want to give a continuing yes to the invitation to come to God in love, and we want to open ourselves to what God wants to do in us to transform us by the Spirit's power into a greater likeness of God in Christ.

In carrying out some element of our pattern of life, we should remind ourselves that we thereby are saying yes to God and asking the Spirit to work in and through us to make us into what God has called us to be. Certainly, the other aspects of our life also should be a yes to God and open us to the Spirit's transforming power, but selecting specific elements that we promise to perform faithfully on a regular basis assures us that there are times when we will consciously call to mind our yes and our openness.

The discipline that the pattern of life imposes helps to strengthen our wills and commitment. It provides some stability in our spiritual practices so that we do not flit from one practice to another looking for spiritual "highs" in the latest fads. The pattern of life also creates a measure of accountability: Have we done what we said we would do? Our pattern of life should create an intentional awareness of our spirituality and our relationship with God.

If we are under spiritual direction, the pattern of life also creates a baseline for discussion in sessions with our director, even if nothing special seems to have happened otherwise. A failure to keep a pattern of life may itself indicate problems that need attention. Are we too busy to take time for ourselves to listen to God? Is our ministry scattered over so many areas that we are jacks-of-all-trades and masters of none? Is our intellectual life stagnating?

It therefore may be helpful to pick some specific aspect of our ministry to be part of our pattern of life for the sake of discipline, focus on our relationship with God, and overall accountability.

OTHER ELEMENTS IN A PATTERN OF LIFE

Although the basic elements of a pattern of life are prayer, study, and ministry, other elements may, and sometimes should, be added. For example, a pastor who knows that he or she needs to keep more physically fit might include a certain amount of exercise as part of a pattern of life. Such exercise is, of course, also a prayer if carried out with the intention of remaining physically fit in order to serve God better.

Here are four examples of health-related actions that could be elements in a pattern of life:

- Take a daily two-mile walk.
- Consume no more than two thousand calories a day.
- Avoid high-cholesterol foods.
- Get a thorough physical examination once a year.

If a minister has not been getting enough sleep, the pattern could require getting eight hours of sleep a night, five nights a week. If the minister is having trouble finding quality time to spend with his or her spouse, the pattern might require taking two week-long vacations a year with the spouse away from the pressures of the church and keeping two evenings a week free for family activities.

A PATTERN OF LIFE AND A SPIRITUALITY

A spirituality can serve as the focal point of spiritual formation, that is, the development and practice of a pattern of life that will enable God to work most effectively in and through us. Spirituality is that aspect of my faith that serves to guide me in how I conduct my life. It is the framework within which I operate in my desire to be faithful to God. It is the principal theme of my relationship with God, something that motivates me and stimulates me toward greater love of and service to God and neighbor.

If you know what your spirituality is, then your pattern of life is best inspired and shaped by that spirituality. If you are unsure about what your spirituality is, then you should ask yourself some questions to clarify what it might be. These questions might include the following:

- What aspect of Christ's work am I most enthusiastic in doing? To what aspect would I most want to devote my time in preference to all others?
- What truth of my faith most inspires me? What truth of my faith do I most enjoy sharing with others? Is there a faith idea or concept that I find especially appealing and that I like to dwell upon and reflect on during my quiet time?
- Is there a person from my past, perhaps a teacher or mentor or relative, who I thought led an exceptionally holy life? If so, what attributes did this person have that I would like to model in my own life? What about this person particularly inspired me toward greater love of God?
- Are there particular pictures or Scripture passages that I find especially moving or motivating? What is it about these pictures or passages that attracts me to them? How can I integrate those insights into my pattern of life?

The purpose of these questions is to elicit the aspect of your faith that is your core theme, the aspect that genuinely excites you, the aspect that can be the centerpiece of your ministry even though your ministry necessarily involves unrelated work as well.

If you still cannot identify your spirituality, do not be discouraged. You are likely to identify a spirituality after practicing your pattern of life for a while. It is the pattern of life that is most important, not the spirituality. A spirituality can be an aid in forming a pattern of life, but it is not absolutely necessary. The pattern itself creates a process that probably will lead to your defining your spirituality.

One possible aid in defining your spirituality as well as developing an appropriate pattern of life is to go on a retreat under the guidance of a spiritual director. The director can provide readings and in-person dialogue to help you clarify your ideas and order your spiritual priorities. By examining your top priorities, you will probably be able to identify your own personal spirituality.

TO SUM IT UP

We can think of spiritual formation as building a house. The psalmist says, "Unless the Lord builds the house, those who build it labor in vain" (Psalm 127:1). We must cooperate as the Lord builds us, that is, draws us more fully into God's own life.

Our pattern of life is the foundation of the house. It consists of those particular practices by which we will accept God's invitation to let the Spirit transform us more into the likeness of Christ, and through which we intentionally remind ourselves that we must be open to God's work in and through us to enable that transformation.

Our spirituality is the frame of the house. The floor plan,

the layout of the rooms, and more are determined by the frame. So too our spirituality provides guidance and the patterns for our ministry and personal growth. The completion of the house is up to God. God is the master builder, but through our pattern of life grounded in our spirituality, we cooperate with God as best we can.

We are not, however, passive participants in what must be done. Cooperating with God means fidelity to what we believe is God's will for us, discipline in keeping our pattern of life, zeal in our ministry, and relating to and communicating with God through prayer. In the next three chapters we will consider two important forms of prayer that help us open ourselves more fully to God's grace: meditation and contemplation. These are among the tools available to help us work alongside God to complete our spiritual house.

7

MEDITATION

WHAT IS MEDITATION?
Human beings are endowed with a variety of faculties by which they acquire and process information. Each one of our senses accesses data of a particular kind and transmits that data to the brain. The brain, in turn, draws on the memory to relate the new data to past experience. Thus, when we taste some food that we have never eaten before, we might say, for example, that it tastes like chicken, or that the sauce contains lemon, because our memories have stored the tastes of chicken and lemon and we can use this stored data to draw conclusions about a new dish.

In addition to our senses, we have emotions or feelings, and we have mental abilities that include will, memory, and reason (reason includes what we normally call understanding). Each of our faculties—sensory, emotional, and mental—interacts with the others. Essentially all information about the world and our bodies comes through the senses, but it is our mental faculties that sift through the avalanche of data and organize it so that we can "make sense" of it. Our emotions tell us how we feel about the information that our mental faculties process, feelings that often prompt us to action, such as flight when the information makes us afraid, or tears when the information makes us sad.

Our senses, of course, cannot provide direct access to God. We cannot taste, smell, hear, touch, or see God as God is. When God chose to appear to Abraham, for example, God had to assume a form that Abraham's senses could perceive. Even Jesus' disciples did not see God the Son. They saw the man Jesus in whom God the Son resided. Only in Jesus' transfiguration did three startled and terrified disciples get a glimpse of Jesus' divine glory. But even then they did not see God fully, because they would have died if they had. Scripture reminds us that no one in this life can look on the face of God—that is, see God as God is—and live (Exodus 33:20; cf. Genesis 32:30; 1 Corinthians 13:12; Revelation 22:4). The physical body could not survive such an experience.

The sensory, emotional, and mental faculties are the tools of prayer. In one sense, the will is the highest faculty because by it we choose to act in accordance with God's will. Love of God is expressed primarily through the will, but we use reason and memory to come to an understanding of what God's will is for us. Our senses also help us to discern God's will—for example, sight and hearing as we read or listen to the divine words of Scripture.

Prayer takes many forms. Every moment of our lives should be a time of prayer. Our lives themselves should be a prayer. Some forms of prayer involve telling God about our needs, our thoughts, our emotions. The psalms are filled with outpourings of the heart to God; they span the whole range of human emotions in addition to voicing deep human concerns and needs. The psalms are models for communicating verbally with God.

Other forms of prayer are times of simply being with God. (We will see more about such prayer in the next two chapters.) But a form of prayer that uses memory and reason to open our hearts and minds to God is meditation. In fact, I define meditation as the act of directing one's attention to God and matters of faith using memory and reason. Through meditation we hope that God will teach us and strengthen us to belong more completely to God. How, then, do we approach the prayerful art of meditation?

PERSONALITY AFFECTS HOW WE MEDITATE

No two human beings are alike, and so people use various methods to meditate. Some people depend more on their emotions and intuition than on their reason to decide whether something is true. These persons we may call intuitive. By contrast, other people are more intellectually oriented and may rarely experience strong emotions. Some people, such as artists and writers, are highly sensitive to their surroundings. They readily pick up colors and shapes, what others are saying and feeling, and how objects relate to one another. We may call these persons sensate. Again by contrast, other people are almost oblivious to their surroundings. After ten years of marriage, they still have trouble remembering the color of their spouse's eyes.

I am not suggesting that sensate persons are better than those who are not or that intuitives are superior to nonintuitives. We are the way we are, and our prayer life must be geared to the way we are. A highly intellectual person is not likely to be attracted to a form of prayer that has a strongly emotional content.

People also differ in the way they think. Some people are highly visual. They think in terms of images and pictures. When they hear the word "dog," they may see a mental image of a dog. Others are more verbal. These folks think primarily with words. When they hear the word "dog," they may bring to mind a set of statements that define a dog. Once again, I am not making a value judgment. There is nothing wrong with being visual and nothing wrong with being verbal. The world needs both kinds of people. Artists are likely to be visual and writers are likely to be verbal.

No one, however, is purely visual or purely verbal; we are speaking only in terms of general tendencies. But both the temperament and thought processes of an individual can play key roles in how that person prays in general and meditates in particular. Visual people are more likely to use images in meditation, and verbal people are more likely to use word descriptions or discourse in their meditations.

TECHNIQUES FOR MEDITATION
Meditation involves directing one's attention to God and matters of faith using memory and reason. At first glance, this may seem to contradict the distinction that I made between two types of people: visually oriented and verbally oriented. However, we construct mental images using the memory. Our imagination is centered in our memory because it is from the memory that we draw the pictures that constitute our visual images. If we had no memory, we would have to rely solely on what our senses are experiencing at the moment. We literally would live from moment to moment with no recollection of past experiences.

Meditation techniques vary in two basic ways: (1) which faculties we use to inspire, or enter into, our meditation; and (2) which faculties we use during the meditation itself.

THE SENSES INSPIRE MEDITATION
Meditation involves the use of memory and intellect to reflect on some aspect of God or our faith. Usually, we first need an inspiration or "trigger" to bring to mind something on which

to meditate. The senses can provide us with such inspiration.

The psalmist remarks, *"The earth is the Lord's and the full-ness thereof"* (Psalm 24:1). God created the universe, and so the universe reveals, although dimly, the glory of God. When we admire a glowing sunset or marvel at the sparkling stars in the evening sky, we may easily be led to reflect on the power and grandeur of the One who created these wonders. Here the inspiration for a meditation comes from the sense of sight. We look at some portion of creation and let our minds soar beyond what we see to what we cannot see.

Sight is but one sense that might lead us to meditation. Touching the soft petals of a flower or the face of an infant or someone we love can cause us to think about God or some wonderful aspect of our faith. Hearing a magnificent symphony or a moving hymn can lead us to meditation. In a similar way, taste and smell may serve as stimuli for meditation.

Once we have entered the meditation using one or more senses to inspire the session, on what, then, will we reflect? The answer, of course, will vary from individual to individual. Even how the meditation proceeds will vary from one person to the next.

We may imagine God in the act of creating the "firmament of heaven" and the stars. We may reflect on how humans are called to share in creation through art and music. We may ponder the powerful intelligence that underlies the universe. We will reflect on whatever our source of inspiration leads us to reflect on. And we may use either mental images or verbal reflections. We may even be silent in the awesome presence of God, not wishing even to think. That is all right, too. We are making ourselves available to God by just being present.

Looking at the beauty of the night sky or listening to a moving song, we may burst out in spontaneous praise of God. Such praise is more than appropriate; we have many examples of such prayer in the Book of Psalms. Strictly speaking, this prayer is not meditation, because it is not using memory or intellect for ˌreflection. But meditation may lead to such prayer, and such prayer may lead to meditation. Once we have declared our praise to God for such glorious works, for example, we may then be led to reflect in silence on God's goodness, righteousness, holiness, or omnipotence.

OTHER SOURCES TO INSPIRE MEDITATION

We might truthfully say that all inspiration for meditation begins with the senses. Even if we find our inspiration in a passage of Scripture, we are using sight to read the passage. But here it is not the sight, sound, taste, smell, or touch of the thing being sensed that is the primary inspiration, but rather, the content. Thus, a melody, through our sense of hearing, can serve to inspire meditation, or the words set to that melody may actually be the inspiration. In the latter case, it is the content or meaning of the words that is the inspiration.

A Scripture passage often can be a springboard to meditation, but for this to happen, the passage must be read slowly and thoughtfully, and then reread until the reader is inspired to reflect on something that the passage brings to mind.

An emotion can be an inspiration for meditation, just as it can be for other forms of prayer. If we are particularly happy, we may reflect on the joy of having Jesus as our savior and brother. If we are apprehensive or fearful, we may reflect on God as our protector and fortress. A picture of Jesus, or a crucifix, or some other sacred object also can stimulate a spirit of meditation.

Note that there is a difference between meditation, which is reflection on or thinking about some aspect of our faith, and prayer, which communicates our thoughts to God. Thus, happiness may lead us to praise God, while fear may lead us to plead for God's help, as well as providing the inspiration for reflection.

IMAGINATIVE AND DISCURSIVE MEDITATION

As noted earlier, some people primarily think visually, while others are more verbal. Visual thinkers tend to prefer "imaginative" meditation, that is, meditation using mental images, while verbal thinkers generally prefer "discursive" meditation, that is, meditation based more on words. There are forms of meditation, however, that include images and dialogue both.

IMAGINATIVE MEDITATION In imaginative meditation, the prayer brings to mind images related to the subject of the meditation. Some examples will help. The inspiration for the examples is Jesus' command "Let the little children come to me."

We might visualize this scene with our mind's eye. Jesus is surrounded by some of his disciples. Is he sitting or standing? That is up to you. You are creating the scene from your imagination. Are they in an open field or close to a house? That too is up to you. Put as many details as you wish in the scene. Once you have placed Jesus there with his disciples, imagine some mothers trying to push through the ring of disciples with their children so they can ask Jesus to bless their children.

The scene is not static like a portrait. It is dynamic. The mothers and children are in motion. The disciples are trying to keep them at a distance from Jesus. Jesus gently beckons to the mothers to bring their children to him. He blesses the children. How does he bless them? Once again, that is for your imagination to decide, but do not try too hard to direct your imagination. Give it free play. Let it lead you where it will.

Instead of being just an observer of what is taking place, you might become a participant. Do you want to be one of the disciples? Perhaps you would rather be one of the mothers bringing a child to Jesus, or be one of the children. You might even place yourself in the role of Jesus blessing little children as they come to you.

As you reflect on the action of the scene, open your mind to whatever message God may want to give you. Are you struck most by the faith of the mothers, by the compassion of Jesus, by the obtuseness of the disciples, or by the simplicity of the children?

In a purely imaginative, or visual, meditation, you do not try to hear what the actors are saying, but there is no reason not to add some dialogue if you so wish. As you are observing the scene in your imagination, you might hear the disciples rebuking the mothers, the children asking who Jesus is, the mothers pleading with Jesus to bless their children, or Jesus pronouncing a blessing.

You can also play the role of one of the actors, you yourself speaking in that role. You might come to Jesus as a little child asking him to bless you and teach you whatever you need to know to grow more fully in love. You might place yourself in the role of Jesus pronouncing a blessing on little children. Do not force words from any of the characters. Let them be free to speak so that you might hear what God wants you to hear.

DISCURSIVE MEDITATION The foregoing examples draw heavily on the imagination to picture the scene and to place ourselves in it. Imagination also plays a key role if we create speech as well as a visual image. Discursive meditation, however, does not use imagination, but reason. We use reason to dialogue with ourselves in trying to learn what the inspiration for our meditation might teach us. Again the inspiration for the examples will be Jesus' command "Let the little children come to me."

In discursive meditation we ask ourselves questions and then try to answer them, keeping our minds as open as possible to whatever lessons God might want us to learn. Here are some questions that Jesus' command might bring to mind:

• Why does Jesus care so deeply for the little children? What characteristic of little children might be particularly appealing to Jesus? Which of those characteristics do I need to foster in myself?

• Am I as a minister bringing my parishioners to Jesus as a mother might bring her children? What blessings do I want Jesus to give my parishioners?

• Am I ever like one of the disciples, pushing away people who want to come to Jesus because they come in a way that makes me uncomfortable? Do I need to change my attitudes so that I can be more open to alternative ways that people can approach Jesus?

THE FREEDOM TO EXPERIMENT

You should feel free to experiment with different forms of meditation to find one that best fits your own temperament and thought patterns. The following suggestions may be helpful to make a meditation session easier and more productive:

• Say a short prayer before starting the meditation to ask God's guidance and protection as you meditate.

• Conclude a session with a prayer that summarizes what you have learned or what you want help with based on what you experienced during the session.

• Find a quiet place where you are not likely to be interrupted and make yourself as comfortable as possible while you meditate in order to minimize distractions. The lotus position may be wonderful for yogis, but I get leg cramps just thinking about it. Leg cramps are a serious obstacle to meditation.

• Do not hesitate to repeat the same form of meditation or use the same source of inspiration for several sessions. The question is not whether you are repeating yourself but whether you are still learning from what you are repeating.

• Try to be alert and fresh when you meditate. Do not save your meditation until you are dog-tired at the end of a busy day. Do not try to squeeze meditation in right before an important meeting, when your mind is more likely to be on that meeting than on anything else. This might lead you to examine how you schedule your time. Is your schedule an obstacle to faithful observance of your pattern of life?

OBJECTIONS TO MEDITATION

As most ministers know, meditation is an important prayer technique in almost every religion of the world, including traditional non-Christian religions, such as Buddhism and Hinduism, and also New Age religions. Because of this, some Christians object to the use of meditation.

Meditation, however, has a long tradition within both Western and Eastern Christianity, particularly, though not exclusively, in monasticism. Prayer, generally, is an integral part of any and every religion, but we do not refuse to pray because non-Christians also pray. If we refuse to have anything to do with any idea or object that is used, has been used, or even has origins in a non-Christian religion, then we will have little left to our Christianity.

Another objection raised against meditation is that the devil may try to deceive us by planting false thoughts in our minds as we meditate, or that we may deceive ourselves, seeing what we want to see or hearing what we want to hear rather than learning what God teaches us in the Scriptures.

First, let me state emphatically that meditation is not meant to be a method to induce visions or voices from heaven. Anyone who starts having visions or hearing voices had better have a good spiritual director or a good psychiatrist, or both. Meditation is nothing more or less than trying to reflect more deeply on aspects of our faith. If we enter meditation with a humble heart, asking God to protect us from error, we are unlikely to fall prey to demons or even to self-deceptions.

We would do well in any case to have a good spiritual director or spiritual companion with whom we can discuss the thoughts that come to us during meditation, as this may help us to clarify whatever ideas come to us and serve as a guard against possible errors.

Meditation is a powerful prayer technique that clergy should not be afraid to use or recommend to parishioners.

8

CONTEMPLATIVE PRAYER
(PART 1)

WHAT IS CONTEMPLATIVE PRAYER? In meditation we use our mental faculties to reflect on aspects of our faith. We initiate meditation and are actively engaged in what happens during meditation. We set the scene in our imaginations or decide what questions to consider. God may intervene during meditation by giving us insights to help us, but we ourselves are doing most of the "work" when we meditate. Meditation is active prayer. Contemplation is resting prayer. I define contemplation as a quiet resting in God.

To understand why we might be interested in contemplation, we need to remember that our destiny as Christians is to come to the knowledge of God through Christ by the power of the Holy Spirit. However, the knowledge of God is not something we can attain by our own efforts. We can use our imaginations to construct a scene based on some scriptural event. We can imagine Christ speaking words from the Gospels. But no amount of effort on our part can bring to mind an accurate image of God. If we construct an image of God, we are, in effect, building an idol. When Paul notes, "No eye has seen, nor ear heard . . . what God has prepared for those who love him" (1 Corinthians 2:9), he is telling us that our senses cannot bring us the direct experience of God, which is what has been prepared for those who love God.

You might agree completely with what I have just said but still ask, "What does this have to do with our prayer life here on earth? We can come to the knowledge of God in due time after we die. Here on earth we have a relationship with God through Jesus, and there is no need for a direct experience of God." We may not think that we have any reasonable expectation that God would give us such an experience in this life anyway, even though Jesus told us that the kingdom of God already has come among us (Luke 17:21).

Certainly, it is true that we cannot experience God fully in this life. We cannot look into the face of God and live. But God does allow us to have a foretaste of the fuller experience of heaven, just as Jesus allowed his disciples to glimpse his divine glory in the transfiguration.

I agree completely that contemplative prayer is not required for salvation, or even for a truly holy life. Our faithfulness to God depends on the choices we make, not on the fervor or style of our prayer. If we are doing our best to please God and to live in accordance with what we believe is God's will, then we are living as we should. But every minister should at least be familiar with the notion of contemplative prayer, even if he or she chooses not to practice it. Here are some reasons why:

- There is substantial interest among Christians today in contemplative prayer. The books and lectures of teachers such as Father Thomas Keating and Dom Lawrence Freeman have helped popularize various forms of contemplative prayer, and therefore it is likely that some of your parishioners are interested in such prayer.
- There is ample evidence that many Christians do have some direct experience of God, and this experience is

sometimes life-changing. It can also be frustrating or frightening because it cannot be communicated to anyone else—if the experience can be described, it is not a direct experience of God—and the one experiencing it does not know what to make of it.

• Frequently, people having direct experiences of God are afraid to bring them to their ministers because they think they will be ridiculed, or be warned that their wonderful experience came from the devil, or be misunderstood as to what they are talking about (which is, alas, all too often the case). Ministers should, therefore, have some knowledge about contemplative prayer so that they can more adequately advise their parishioners who are involved with it.

You may argue that you and your parishioners are not engaged in contemplative prayer, but my guess is that many of your parishioners are engaged in it and do not want to talk about it with you because they fear a negative reaction. If you yourself are unwilling to explore contemplative prayer with an open mind, then you should find someone you trust who is willing to learn about it and to whom you can refer parishioners with questions about it.

ACTIVE CONTEMPLATIVE PRAYER

There are two basic forms of contemplative prayer: active and passive. Contemplative prayer is a quiet resting in God. In active contemplation, we initiate the prayer; in passive contemplation, the initiative is God's.

In a session of active contemplative prayer we wish to make our soul as directly available to God as we can. What interferes with our being directly available to God? Mental and sensory distractions. If our mind is focused on Sunday's sermon, or even if we are working at constructing a mental image of Christ on the cross, we are occupied with something other than being directly available to God.

We are, of course, directly available to God at all times in the sense that God can do whatever God pleases with us—speak to us directly or even lift us off the ground! But, fortunately or unfortunately, such events are highly unusual, for ministers or for anyone else.

In active contemplation we try to put aside all mental and sensory distractions so that our soul can be as directly available to God as possible. An analogy may help. Think of your soul as a container and God as a precious ointment. We want our container to be filled with the precious ointment, but when we are distracted, it gets filled with some common material such as water. When we engage in active contemplation, we try to dump out all of the water so that our container has room for the precious ointment.

We want to get rid of distractions, so we want to reduce our mental and physical activity to a minimum. How do we do this? Several techniques are commonly used, the most popular probably being that promoted by Fathers Thomas Keating and M. Basil Pennington, both Trappist monks.

THE METHOD OF KEATING AND PENNINGTON If you are to reduce mental and physical distractions to a minimum, you need to be in a location that is as free of distractions as possible. A quiet room where you are not likely to be interrupted is a good start. A familiar room rather than a strange room is even better, so that you are not distracted by trying to become acquainted with your surroundings. Next, you should get yourself as comfortable as possible. You may get so comfortable that you become afraid that you might fall asleep. That is okay. Sometimes people do go to sleep when they engage in centering prayer. Father Keating teaches that if you fall asleep, you probably need the sleep more than you need the centering prayer.

Next, pick what Father Keating calls a "sacred word." The word should be short—one or two syllables—and it should have special meaning for you, something like "love," "God," or "Jesus." This word is not a mantra. You are selecting this word for this session only, and you are not supposed to keep repeating it over and over again. How, then, is the sacred word used?

The sacred word is used to prevent distractions from interfering with keeping our soul directly open to God. If a concern about an upcoming meeting enters our thoughts, we gently use the sacred word to deflect it. If we were to concentrate on avoiding distractions, that effort itself would become a major distraction. So we ignore such distractions in the same way that we would ignore traffic noise outside. When a distraction seems to be gaining our attention, we use the sacred word to deflect it. The sacred word is not a shield. It is more like a feather used to divert a pesky insect away from us. We should not change the sacred word during the session, because thinking of a new word would itself be a distraction.

When we choose the sacred word, we should recall that we are renewing our yes to the invitation to come to God in love, and we want to be open to God's grace to transform us into the fullness of what God invites us to become. That is why we try to make our soul directly available to God in centering prayer without physical or mental distractions. We offer ourselves as directly to God as possible and implicitly ask God's will to be done with us. However, during the centering prayer itself, we do not try to bring these intentions consciously to mind, because that too would be a distraction.

Will God, in fact, do anything when we engage in centering prayer? God is always acting in us if we are open to God's action. Some people practice centering prayer because they think that it is a quick path to passive contemplation (discussed below). This is not the best reason for centering prayer, although passive contemplation may be a desirable goal provided that we ask for it so that we can become more completely God's and not as an end in itself. Some people use centering prayer as a method to relax, and it is an excellent technique for many simply to become calm, cool, and collected.

But whether God does anything overtly during centering prayer or not, the important thing is that we are making ourselves available to God. We are trying to make our souls available to God. Certainly, that is a valid prayer.

As with meditation, there may be some fear of deception. We cannot avoid the possibility of deception in any activity that we undertake. All we can do is place ourselves humbly in the hands of the God who loves us, the God who is all truth, and pray that God will not allow us to fall prey to the forces of evil. If we refuse to meditate or engage in active contemplation because we are afraid that a demon might use the opportunity to gain control of our mind or soul, then we should reexamine our attitudes about Jesus and the power he has over all demonic forces. Yes, we can be deceived, but if we have such little trust in God that we are afraid that a sincere attempt to open ourselves to God's grace and love will be, or can be, preempted by demonic forces more powerful than God, then we already have been deceived.

OTHER METHODS OF ACTIVE CONTEMPLATION

Whatever technique we use as a means to enter active contemplation, a quiet resting in God is directed toward reducing or eliminating distractions so that the soul can be as totally available directly to God as possible. We touch briefly on four additional techniques. If you wish to learn more about any of them, ample literature is available.

THE METHOD OF DOM LAURENCE FREEMAN Dom Laurence is an English Benedictine monk who teaches a method of centering prayer developed by his fellow monastic John Miles. Father Miles got his method from having lived for a time in a Hindu ashram. Instead of a sacred word, one chooses a mantra (this is the term used by Dom Laurence, so I will use it, too). Dom Laurence suggests "maranatha" (found in 1 Corinthians 16:22, Aramaic for "Our Lord, come!") as a good mantra. This form of centering prayer is, therefore, essentially a "baptized" version of a Hindu practice, but there is nothing wrong in taking good ideas from other religions, interpreting them in Christian terms, and using them in the service of our Lord Jesus Christ.

The mantra is repeated again and again. It is the constant repetition that helps the mind become empty of extraneous thoughts.

THE JESUS PRAYER The Prayer of Silence, or Hesychastic Prayer, which has a long and rich tradition in Eastern Orthodoxy, is commonly known as the Jesus Prayer and is similar in many ways to Dom Laurence's use of a mantra, although this venerable form of prayer has never had any association with a non-Christian religion. A person using the Jesus Prayer repeats over and over in a barely audible tone the sentence "Lord Jesus Christ, Son of God, have mercy on me, a sinner." Some practitioners shorten the words to "Jesus, have mercy" or simply to "Jesus."

The Jesus Prayer, repeated over and over throughout the day, is intended to bring about a change of heart. It is not prayer intended for use within a time-limited session, like centering prayer. Rather, the spirit of the prayer, by constant repetition throughout the day, is to permeate the entire life of the person using it and ultimately to bring about what the

Eastern Orthodox call the Prayer of the Heart, which is a close union of the person's life with the life of God.

LECTIO DIVINA, OR HOLY READING Holy Reading, like the Jesus Prayer, is intended to effect a conversion of life more than to induce a state of active or passive contemplation, although that is what many people try to use it for today. As the name implies, Holy Reading involves reading Scripture (usually), but reading slowly, thoughtfully, and with an open heart. If some word or phrase speaks in a special way to the reader, he or she meditates (in the sense described in chapter 7) on that word or phrase. During Holy Reading special attention is paid to what God might be trying to teach the reader through what is read.

After meditating on the special word or phrase, the reader is led to pray, the prayer being inspired by the meditation itself. From this prayer, the reader may then enter into a time of quiet resting in God, that is, contemplation. The four steps—reading, meditation, prayer, and contemplation—sometimes are called "Guigo's Ladder," after the twelfth-century Carthusian monk who first described them.

THE PRAYER OF BEING PRESENT TO GOD We may not need to use any special technique to be present to God and to enter a state of active contemplation. When we deeply love someone, it often suffices simply to be with that person. We do not feel that we must carry on a conversation; just being together is sufficient to make us content. So it is with God. If we remind ourselves that God is ever present to us and loves us, we can sit quietly and be there for God while God is there for us, lovers present to one another. When distractions come, we simply remind ourselves that God is with us and we are with God. Our desire is to be open to God in these times and to affirm by our availability to God that we want more than anything else to belong fully to God.

WHAT IF NONE OF THESE WORK?

Just as someone may find meditation difficult, so too someone may find that none of the methods of active contemplative prayer seems to do any good. Distractions are overpowering. God seems more distant during a session of centering prayer than when we are busy counseling a parishioner in our office.

My advice to any Christian is to use the form of prayer that works best. One does not have to be "successful" at meditation or contemplation in order to love God. In Scripture we are commanded to love God in fullness of heart and soul and mind and strength. Nowhere does Scripture say that we must engage in centering prayer or discursive meditation. Nevertheless, these can be significant spiritual aids for many prayerful people.

Two basic questions are these: How do I know if a certain form of prayer works for me? What is prayer supposed to do for me if it works?

God looks first at the heart, not the results of our efforts. Prayer of any sort in times of dryness and desolation may have more spiritual value than a torrent of prayer when we are feeling content and energetic. Hard choices that are in accord with what we believe to be God's will bring us closer to union with God than easy choices that agree with what we really want to do anyway. Therefore, we should not judge the quality of prayer by how good it makes us feel.

Jesus said, "By their fruits you will know them," and this test applies as well to prayer as to anything else. If our prayer is leading us to greater fidelity to God's will and less concern with our own preferences, if our prayer is bringing about the signs of a sound spiritual foundation, if our prayer is making us recognize our utter dependence on God in our ministry, then our prayer is working, regardless of how it "feels."

Even our honest anger at God because we feel that God is far away or has even abandoned us is a prayer. It demonstrates to God that we truly care about our relationship. There is no love when we cannot care enough to be angry, and we may learn from our anger what still remains to be healed in our relationship with God.

Our lives are to be continual affirmations of our desire to be joined to God in love and open to God's work within and through us. When we are, by the grace of God, functioning in that mode, our entire life becomes a prayer. As we die to self in order that Christ might live more completely in us, we will experience a sense of loss. All deaths are painful. We must sur-render control of our life to God, and that is never easy. If our prayer helps us to surrender, it is working.

9

CONTEMPLATIVE PRAYER
(PART 2)

*P*ASSIVE CONTEMPLATION

If you do not believe that God will provide anyone a direct experience of Godself, however incomplete and dim in this life, you may skip this chapter. On second thought, probably you had better read it. Too many solid Christians have had what they were sure was a direct experience of God to dismiss the matter lightly. And many Christians who have had such an experience are reluctant to discuss it with their ministers because they are afraid that they will not be understood (their experience of God is indescribable) or that what was one of the most profound events of their lives will be belittled.

Mysticism generally is not in vogue in Christianity today, but this is due more to its being misunderstood than because it is contrary to Scripture or tradition. Someone has a mystical experience when he or she has a direct encounter with God rather than one mediated through symbols or other created beings, including other people.

Using mysticism in this sense, we find many examples of mysticism in Scripture: God's appearances to Moses in the burning bush and on Sinai, Elijah's encounter with God on Horeb, Jesus' transfiguration, and Paul's transport to the "third heaven" for an experience that he could not put into words. There have been great mystics in both Eastern and Western Christianity, including the two most important writers on mystical prayer, John of the Cross and Teresa of Avila.

In active contemplation, the person praying seeks to remove all mental and physical distractions so that he or she can be completely available to God, to become an empty vessel, so to speak, that God can fill. In passive contemplative prayer, God takes the initiative and gives the soul a direct experience of Godself.

When I speak of direct experience, I am not saying that God completely reveals the Divine Being to anyone in this life. Nor is it the case that God gives direct experiences of Godself in the same way or to the same degree to everyone, or even to the same person. Just as a rheostat can control the intensity of a spotlight, so too God controls the extent to which a soul will be allowed to see the Divine Being.

Because God alone can grant passive contemplation, it is a free gift of God. God chooses to whom and to what degree such revelations occur. But one point should be clear. Passive contemplative prayer is not a requirement for holiness of life, which, as I said before, consists of conforming our wills to God's will for us. Passive contemplative prayer often gives powerful assistance for spiritual growth, but it is not required for such growth. What is required, of course, is cooperation with the grace of God. But God gives us those gifts we need to grow more completely into God's own life, and not necessarily those gifts we would like to have. Those who have known the joy and peace that come with a direct experience of God would like to continue that experience every moment of every day since it is nothing less than a foretaste of heaven, but that is a favor that God rarely if ever grants to anyone in this life.

THE DARK NIGHT OF THE SENSES

In passive contemplation God is not experienced directly by our thoughts, emotions, or senses, but by our souls. Consequently, when God begins a direct, but dim, self-revelation to the soul, our natural faculties cannot participate in the experience, although they will be affected. The intellect, which wants to understand and describe, may be confused and distressed because what is taking place is both indescribable and incomprehensible. The emotions and senses, also bypassed by passive contemplation, may clamor for attention.

The active prayer techniques—talking to God, meditation, and active contemplation—will fail in periods of passive contemplation because they depend on our use of our natural faculties, whereas God is acting directly on the soul. Forms of prayer that previously came easily for us and brought consolation and joy will prove difficult or impossible. We will feel as if we have entered a desert of prayer, a dry inability to pray. It is not that we do not want to pray. We simply cannot pray. We cannot pray, because God is "praying us." The soul's attention is absorbed by God so that attempts to use our natural faculties in prayer meet with frustration.

Whether or not this difficult period, when our usual forms of prayer no longer seem to work, is actually the result of the stirring of passive contemplation, it is an important stage in our spiritual development. We must, at some point, recognize that all of the mental images of God we have constructed and all of the emotional rewards we have gained from our self-initiated prayer are not God. If we become too attached to anything that is not God, it becomes an idol for us, a false god, even without our being consciously aware that this has happened.

Ultimately, we must give up whatever we have within us that separates us from God. We must love God totally, completely, absolutely; that is, we must belong to God in every aspect of our being. Only God can make this happen, but for it to happen, we must be willing to let God remove those obstacles that keep it from happening. Often, one of those obstacles is an attachment to something that originally was a spiritual aid but now has become something to which we are attached for its own sake. The "letting go" of such attachments can bring emotional pain and anxiety.

This period of dryness during which our willingness to follow God for God's own sake is tested and strengthened is sometimes called "the dark night of the senses." It is a night when the senses, and the mind and emotions as well, are darkened, perhaps blinded by the powerful light of God, which is not recognized as such, or perhaps just blinded, so that we might better see with the eyes of faith. Blessed are those who have not seen and yet believe (John 20:29).

STAGES OF SPIRITUAL GROWTH

If God is at work transforming us, drawing us more and more into God's own life, we should expect there to be identifiable milestones in this process. Is there a way to determine how far along God already has brought us?

In one sense, the answer is no. The real test of our transformation is how fully our wills have been converted into the will of Christ. Just as Christ's human perfection rested in his always being faithful to his Father's will, so our perfection rests in how closely our wills coincide with the will of Christ in our own individual characteristics and circumstances.

On the other hand, how we view God may well change, if we will allow it to change, during this process of transformation. At first we may view God primarily as lawgiver and judge. We may suspect that God has a genuine dislike for humans but is willing to save a few of them for the sake of the

Son, who died so that could happen. This suspicion that God abhors humans may be a projection of our awareness of, and anxiety over, our own sinfulness.

This view of God makes us emphasize obedience to God in order to avoid hell and gain heaven. We want to do things right, and so the temptation is legalism: complete obedience to the letter of the law because that is the only way to please God and avoid a horrible eternity.

But as God continues to act within us, we begin to see God more as good per se and as a friend who cares about us and wants to bring us into the glorious divine light. We loosen up in how we approach God. The spirit of the law becomes more important than its letter. We are willing to talk to God as we would talk to a friend. We want to know more about God and please God through good works because we see God as wonderful, someone to please, not to fear.

We then may recognize that God wishes to be more than our friend. God wants to share the Divine Being with us in the same way as in the incarnation—that is, to let us see the "fullness of God" (Colossians 1:19)—and through grace to draw us into divine life. And then, we begin to think of God as lover. We want to be united intimately to God through love, to be conformed to God through Christ by the power of the Holy Spirit with every fiber of our being. We surrender ourselves to God in loving intimacy.

Our spiritual growth essentially lies in "letting go and letting God," as the saying goes. Our life becomes less and less our life and more and more God living in and through us. We no longer seek to control what will happen to us, but rather, we surrender to God's control. This willingness to become vulnerable to God is what removes our fear.

In this granting of absolute control to God, we die to self. Though we maintain our individuality, we become what God

created us to become: other Christs, in a sense, in our con-
formity to God. The incarnation is mirrored in us, not because
we are God as Christ is God, but because we are Christ's
and Christ is ours; and by the grace of God, we share in
Christ's life.

BENEFITS OF PASSIVE CONTEMPLATION

No one has a right to passive contemplation, and it is not
required for spiritual growth, but it is a powerful spiritual aid.
My belief, based on my years of experience as a spiritual director and working in spiritual formation, is that most Christians
do experience passive contemplative prayer at least occasion-
ally, and some experience it quite regularly. Many who have
been so gifted do not talk about it for fear of being dismissed
as imagining their experience or being warned that the devil
was trying to deceive them.

Generally, the fruits of genuine passive contemplative
prayer are a deeper devotion to God and a more intense desire
to serve God. This is true despite the dryness of prayer that a
person might mistake for abandonment by God in the dark
night of the senses.

A person in passive contemplative prayer usually senses
God close at hand but cannot describe either God or what is
happening. Despite the seeming inability to pray in more cus-
tomary ways and the turmoil of the mind, the soul feels at
peace. God's self-revelation is so clear that there is no doubt
on the person's part that it is God. The soul wishes to rest in
God so close at hand and would gladly spend the rest of life in
this state. In even more intense contemplative prayer, the
senses and the mind are stilled by the overpowering presence
of God, and the person praying loses track of time.

Because God is taking the soul by the hand and leading it
gently to a direct experience of the Divine Being, a person in

contemplative prayer cannot act contrary to the will of God in this state. If someone claims to experience contemplative gifts but these gifts bring pride and other forms of sin in their wake, there is good reason for the minister to be suspicious about the authenticity of the gifts.

By allowing the soul to know the Divine Being in contemplative prayer, God is providing a special aid for the soul to grow spiritually. It is much more difficult for anyone who has experienced God directly to make God a lesser priority in his or her life. To have tasted the sweetness of God is better than any earthly pleasure, and someone so gifted can never doubt either the reality of God or the joy that heaven will bring. Having been touched directly by the goodness of God, such a person most likely will find the love of God more passionate and lasting.

But even though the gift of contemplative prayer, particularly in its more intense forms, can bring peace and joy beyond description, the soul should not allow itself to become attached to these gifts in themselves. God alone is the end and goal of our longing, and we must belong completely to God before we can look into the face of God without pain. Hell and heaven both may be nothing more than looking directly into the face of God, but each with a different perspective that makes all the difference. The blessed are one with God in love and feel inexpressible joy at the sight of God's face; the damned are those who, having made themselves their own gods, experience unbearable pain in looking into the face of the one true God, whom they have rejected.

Because God makes more intimate contact with the soul during passive contemplation than during active prayer, contemplative prayer often is deeply desired. Many practitioners of centering prayer hope to use it as a springboard to passive contemplation. But passive contemplation comes at God's own time, if it comes at all. It cannot be turned on and off like a light switch. One knows when it is happening and misses it when it is no longer there, but nothing a person does can make it happen or prolong it once it occurs. Anyone who claims to be able to turn such prayer on and off at will almost certainly is not involved in passive contemplation.

A minister may rightly be wary of reports of special "mystical gifts" such as visions and locutions, the latter where God, Jesus, or a saint literally speaks to someone in prayer. Such unusual events should not be mistaken for passive contemplation. Because they affect the senses and can be described, they are not the direct experience of God.

How should a minister deal with a parishioner who claims to have had a vision or a locution? John of the Cross, one of the great teachers on contemplative prayer, advised his readers to ignore such events. He stated that it is God who must transform the soul, and if someone has unusual experiences of the sort mentioned, then God already has accomplished the purpose for which the visions or locutions were given, and the events can then be safely ignored. To dwell on them is to risk being distracted from a single-minded love of God, because one may come to value the visions and locutions in their own right and not for their spiritual value, if they have any. The devil, of course, can provide "light shows" and apparent locutions to try to lead even the devout astray.

In our attempt to discern true passive contemplation, a humble and experienced spiritual director can be an invaluable asset to guide us through the confusion and anxiety that we may experience as our mental constructs are challenged. A minister might prepare a reference list of spiritual directors, who have been scrutinized for orthodoxy and good reputation, for parishioners who are experiencing passive contemplation or who simply want to explore different forms of prayer.

10

SPIRITUAL DIRECTION

THE BENEFITS OF SPIRITUAL DIRECTION Generally, spiritual growth is more difficult for the person who attempts it on his or her own. Of course we all need the help of the Holy Spirit, but I am not talking even about trying to make progress on one's own with the help of God. Rather, Christians are called to assist one another in their spiritual journeys. The support available from other Christians is an invaluable spiritual aid. What kind of aid can others give? Here are four suggestions:

• Talking with someone about our spiritual practices helps make us accountable. If we have a pattern of life, we are more motivated to maintain it when regularly required to discuss our fidelity to it with someone else. A spiritual director, who is someone with whom we can discuss our spiritual practices, can, therefore, help us remain focused on our spiritual practices and prayer life because he or she will question us about them. The director may ask us to jot down special insights and "God moments" as soon as practicable after they occur so that we can discuss them together. This helps us pay greater attention to how God is acting in our life.

• A spiritual director provides a compassionate ear to help us clarify how God is acting in our life and how we might respond to cooperate most fully with God. This process of discerning what God is doing to teach and transform us is the heart of spiritual direction.

• An experienced spiritual director may recommend books, workshops, prayer techniques, and other resources that might be helpful to us. Although the director does not compel us, he or she does make suggestions and presumably is aware of resources that we may not know about or think of using.

• A spiritual director prays with and for us. The director is more than a guide; he or she is a companion on the journey. The director never should be viewed as an "enlightened one" or "guru," but as a fellow pilgrim whom God has called to help other pilgrims on their way.

Because we are so enmeshed in what happens to us and have so many biases and illusions about ourselves, it often is quite difficult for us to discern what God is doing in our life or how we should respond. We can find spiritual aid in having a compassionate and nonjudgmental listener who also can ask appropriate questions to help us clarify in our mind what is happening with us, and who is sufficiently objective to provide trustworthy evaluations about us. This individual can be of even greater benefit to us if he or she also is experienced in Christian spiritual life and is a person of prayer.

Having seen what a spiritual director is supposed to do and how this might benefit us spiritually, we now will define spiritual direction and distinguish it from psychotherapy and pastoral counseling. Because a spiritual director can benefit pastors and laypersons alike, but pastors sometimes are leery of spiritual direction, I will discuss spiritual direction both for the pastor and for the layperson.

WHAT IS SPIRITUAL DIRECTION?

The primary role of a spiritual director is to assist a "directee" in discerning how God is acting in the directee's life and in formulating an appropriate response to God's action. Such assistance is spiritual direction, and this is its essence: to help the directee identify what God is doing, or trying to do, with the directee and how he or she can best cooperate with God in that work.

Note that the work of the director is to help a directee with discernment. The directee is the one who makes the final decisions both as to what God is doing and how to respond. The director's attitude must be one of humble submission to the Holy Spirit. It must be the Holy Spirit who is working through the director to assist the directee in understanding more clearly how God is leading him or her. A director who attempts to impose his or her own will on a directee or who presumes to be the only one to know what a directee must do to become "holy" can do immense damage because that director is assuming a role that belongs only to God.

A director also may suggest a prayer technique or recommend a book that might benefit the directee. If the technique is tried or the book read, the reactions of the directee then can be discussed, but it is always the directee's decision whether or not to use the technique or read the book, or what to do with any information once it is received.

One must distinguish what a spiritual director does from what pastoral counselors and psychotherapists do, since spiritual direction is neither pastoral counseling nor psychotherapy.

A pastoral counselor assists the counselee in addressing a life issue or responding to a moral dilemma. A pastoral counselor may prepare a couple for marriage or help a parishioner discern a call to ordained ministry. Pastoral counseling is limited in terms of time or issues. Once a life issue or moral predicament has been addressed, or the question has become moot, there is no further need for the pastoral counseling.

Psychotherapists, by definition, deal with clients with adjustment issues or psychological problems. Some mental concern or abnormality has become so disruptive of the client's life that he or she seeks professional help to make life more bearable and, hopefully, normal again. Once the problem, real or imagined, has been resolved to the client's satisfaction, the treatment ends. Here, as with pastoral counseling, the counselor-counselee relationship is formed to deal with a specific issue. Once the issue has been addressed satisfactorily, the relationship is dissolved.

In spiritual direction, the director-directee relationship is not formed with regard to a specific issue or ailment, but because the directee is seeking aid in strengthening his or her relationship with God. The directee wants to grow spiritually and is looking for someone who can help with that growth.

I must mention also that spiritual direction is not confession. The spiritual director does not take the place of the priest in those denominations that have sacramental confession, nor does the spiritual director mediate between the directee and Christ. If a directee has committed sins and is seeking forgiveness, such forgiveness is not sought from the director; rather, the directee relies on the practices of his or her own church. The director, of course, does not want the directee to sin, but sin is not the focus of direction. Sin is, unfortunately, a part of human life, but the directee does not come to the director to find absolution. The director, rather, wants to support the directee in growing into the life and love of God.

The role of spiritual director is a specific calling within the church. It is not a ministry that one chooses for oneself. Often, someone simply comes to the realization that he or she is "doing" spiritual direction. People have been coming to this person for spiritual advice or to tell their special stories of what God is doing in their lives because they sense that he or she is someone who will listen with a compassionate and empathetic ear. Those who come also have a sense that the Holy Spirit is acting in the one they seek out, and they feel safe and comfortable listening to what that person has to say.

By its nature, spiritual direction is a highly personal relationship and involves sharing at the deepest level of a person's life. A certain chemistry is involved that makes the relationship work, a compatibility between director and directee. This implies that a director who is a good fit for one person might not be for another. In general, the first sessions with a potential director should be more like trial meetings to see if there is a good match. Unless both director and directee are comfortable with one another, the relationship will not work.

A pastor may prefer having another pastor as a spiritual director because a pastor is more likely to understand the issues that other pastors face, but laypersons can also make excellent directors for pastors. Laypersons, on the other hand, might discuss matters with their directors that they would not discuss with their pastors. This should not be viewed as distrust of the pastor, much less as an insult. The pastor perhaps is seen as an authority figure, whereas the lay directee is looking for a peer companion on the journey. Also, a directee, particularly if a pastor, may well feel more comfortable with a director who is not a member of the same church and who is not encountered on a regular basis outside of the direction sessions.

Are pastors necessarily spiritual directors as well? I believe, based on my personal observations, that the majority of ministers do not want to be spiritual directors and are not called to be spiritual directors. Spiritual direction can be a time-intensive obligation, time that pastors often do not have. The relationship can last for many years, and the loss of a trusted director with whom a good rapport has been established is like the loss of a dear friend. Pastors often are too mobile to form stable, long-term relationships in one particular locale. Many pastors do see themselves as the "authorities" on spiritual matters and may tend to be more "directive" than a good director should be. A directee may well be more hesitant to challenge the advice of his or her pastor, even when thinking that the pastor is wrong, than to question the advice of a director who is not the pastor.

Spiritual direction is a special ministry within the church. A person might be called to be an ordained minister but not to be a spiritual director. Likewise, a layperson may be a spiritual director without being ordained. But what characteristics should a good spiritual director have?

WHAT MAKES A GOOD SPIRITUAL DIRECTOR?

Here we look at nine attributes that are essential for a good spiritual director.

First, she is a person of prayer who recognizes that she is but God's instrument and that God must work through her if she is to help her directees. Spiritual direction is the work of the Holy Spirit more than it is the work of the director. The director is always praying for guidance both for herself and for her directees.

Second, he is humble in the sense of recognizing that he is helping directees to discern God's path for them, not the path that he would map out for them. He is willing to acknowledge that some directees are in a deeper relationship with God than he is and are receiving greater gifts in prayer than he does. His work really is the work of the Holy Spirit, and when he sees progress in a directee, he thanks God rather than taking pride in himself.

Third, she is experienced in the spiritual life, so she can identify with much of what the directee might talk about. A director who has only read books about prayer is like someone who advertises herself as a flight instructor because she has read a book about airplanes. Good directors passionately seek to love God in every aspect of their being. As a result, a good director is usually receiving spiritual direction herself (see the ninth attribute).

Fourth, he is able to keep confidences. Often, a director is not an ordained minister, and thus may not be bound legally or ethically by the same standards of confidentiality required of clergy, but he keeps them nonetheless. No directee will, or should, trust a director who might reveal his or her innermost thoughts to others without express authorization.

Fifth, she has a strong sense of boundaries. A director does not allow herself to become emotionally or romantically involved with a directee. At best, such involvements could destroy the director's objectivity, and at worst, they could do irreparable harm to directee and director alike. Although a director cares deeply about her directees and loves them in Christ, she retains a distance sufficient enough to enable her to identify areas where the directee needs improvement and to give frank assessments whenever the need for them arises. The director is even able and willing to suggest that the relationship be terminated if she believes that it is no longer productive or that the proper conditions for direction are no longer present.

Sixth, he has sufficient theological knowledge so that he does not inadvertently lead a directee into doctrinal error and is able to recognize such error when it appears. A director intentionally decides which theological viewpoints he is comfortable with. If a directee comes to him with a theological outlook incompatible with his own, the director will probably suggest that the directee find another director who shares his or her point of view.*

Seventh, she knows enough psychology to be able to identify conditions that might require referring a directee to a psychotherapist. Unless the director is also a trained psychotherapist, she should not attempt psychotherapy. Most authorities on spiritual direction recommend that the director not be the directee's therapist as well, although there is nothing to prevent a directee from being in both direction and therapy at the same time.

Eighth, he is not judgmental. The purpose of spiritual direction is to help the directee discern how to respond to God's promptings in his or her life. The director may suggest that certain actions of the directee are destructive to a healthy relationship with God. If the directee continues in behavior that the director cannot countenance as consistent with a sincere desire to cooperate with God, then the director is free to terminate the relationship. The director should not, however, utter condemnations or hurl anathemas.

Ninth, generally a director should be in spiritual direction herself. She also does well to be involved in a peer supervision group or have a consulting director to provide oversight and

---

*The aim of spiritual direction is not proselytization. If, for example, a Buddhist came to me asking for spiritual direction, I would politely decline, because I do not consider myself sufficiently conversant with Buddhism to direct a Buddhist, and I certainly would not use the meeting to try to convert that person to Christianity. Evangelism is a different ministry from spiritual direction. I feel comfortable directing Episcopalians and Roman Catholics, but I would probably decline to direct someone belonging to the Church of Christ. This is not because I consider members of the Church of Christ to be inferior or un-Christian, but simply because I do not understand their ethos sufficiently to be able to relate satisfactorily to a Church of Christ directee. Spiritual directors must be aware of what they know and what they do not know.

accountability in her work as a director and to help her identify and deal with potentially harmful phenomena such as projection and transference.

DOES A DIRECTOR NEED FORMAL TRAINING?

One might well ask if a spiritual director should have special training or be "certified." Currently, there are hundreds of programs in the United States purporting to train spiritual directors. These programs run anywhere from several weeks to three years. There is no accreditation of such training, and no uniform standards have been established. Nor are there "boards" or other examinations to determine the competency of an individual to be a director. One can simply "hang out a shingle" and proclaim oneself to be a director. Nor am I aware of any denominationally based program that licenses, ordains, or certifies directors. Even someone who satisfactorily completes one of the many training programs is not thereby certified, but rather, receives only a certificate of completion.

Many persons who wind up as spiritual directors just find themselves in that role. Once they realize that God has placed them in that role, they may seek further expertise through a formal program or additional reading.

Some ministers want spiritual directors to work only under their supervision. Generally, this does not work. Frequently, the minister does not understand spiritual direction, or is no better trained, and perhaps less well prepared and experienced, in direction than the director. Moreover, the director cannot reveal confidences gained in direction to others, even to his or her pastor. If directees even suspected that what they told the director was being passed on to others, even a member of the clergy, they would hesitate or refuse to enter direction. If the pastor attempts to tell a director how to guide directees, other than demanding high ethical standards, the pastor is assuming the role of the Holy Spirit. Each directee must be handled as an individual.

Spiritual directors should be under direction themselves, and it is also desirable that they be members of peer supervision groups. In a peer supervision group, a director can explore personal emotions and issues related to direction without revealing the confidences of directees. In larger metropolitan areas there are also numerous continuing education opportunities for directors. In addition, national conferences and workshops are held to help directors to network and to sharpen their skills.

If the director is made a member of the pastor's staff, he or she should be covered by liability insurance, but as of this writing, I know of no case in which a director has been sued in that capacity for malfeasance or malpractice.

OBJECTIONS TO SPIRITUAL DIRECTION

I have mentioned several times that spiritual direction can be a spiritual aid to any Christian who sincerely wishes to be found by God. A pastor might want to have readily available a list of trusted spiritual directors to whom he or she can refer parishioners who might benefit from direction. Some pastors, however, are resistant to the concept of spiritual direction. Perhaps they are reluctant to enter direction because they have concerns about whether the practice is consonant with their beliefs. Here is a list of the five most common pastoral objections to spiritual direction (my responses follow the list):

> 1. The Holy Spirit works directly with individuals to guide them spiritually, so there is no need for a human mediator to serve as a director.
>
> 2. I have no control over what the director will say, so the director might give a member of my church ideas that are inconsistent with our doctrine.

3. If anyone is going to direct my parishioners spiritually, it should be me. I am the one ordained to guide my parishioners in their relationship with God.

4. I do not like the term "direction." I do not tell my parishioners what they have to do. I let them prayerfully form their own consciences based on God's word.

5. There are no denominational standards for what it takes to be a spiritual director, no licensing or ordination for this ministry, and no examination to determine if someone is competent to be a spiritual director. Therefore, I am taking a risk in recommending spiritual direction for my parishioners.

The first objection notes that the Holy Spirit is the true spiritual guide of each Christian, so there is no need for a director to serve as a mediator. This objection misunderstands the role of the director. The director is not a mediator between the Holy Spirit and the directee. The Holy Spirit is acting directly on the directee, whereas the director's role is to help the directee recognize what the Spirit is doing and how to respond. The director is an objective "sounding board." Even those who reject any human mediation between an individual and Jesus will admit that Christians can assist one another in their spiritual journeys.

The second objection is that the pastor cannot control what the director might say to the directee. This is true, and it is required if the direction relationship is to work. The pastor might interview potential directors to learn more about them and thus decide whom to recommend to parishioners seeking a director. But just as a director should not try to control a directee, a pastor should not try to control a director. It is the Holy Spirit who must do the work in direction if it is to be successful. If a pastor believes that he or she is the only person in the church through whom the Holy Spirit can work, then there is more of a problem with the pastor than with the spiritual director.

The third objection is made by those pastors who believe that they are the only ones called and qualified to give their members spiritual guidance. They therefore must believe that God acts only through them and that their members are not to minister to one another. Since Sunday school teachers give spiritual guidance, the pastor must either teach every class or outline in detail what a teacher can say. Pastors should be interested in empowering and freeing their members for ministry. At some point a pastor has to trust both the people and the Holy Spirit acting in and through them.

The fourth objection relates to the term "direction." This objection, frequently heard, creates a barrier for some to entering spiritual direction. However, it is a term that has been used for some time. The director might be called a spiritual "guide," but to some, this has New Age connotations that are more threatening than spiritual "director." The terms "spiritual companion" and "soul friend" are sometimes used, but these mean something different from "director," as we will see below. As long as the spiritual director does what a director is supposed to do, if you can find a better title, use it.

The fifth objection notes that there are no denominational standards that one must satisfy before assuming the role of spiritual director. This is indeed the case and is likely to remain so for the foreseeable future. The directee must take responsibility for examining the qualifications and experience of a potential director, and the first two sessions, at least, with a director should be considered trial runs to see if there is a good fit. A pastor, as noted above, also might interview potential directors before deciding whether to recommend them to parishioners.

Perhaps the best way for a pastor to learn more about

spiritual direction is to enter it. A pastor might be hesitant to get spiritual advice from a layperson, but many of the best spiritual directors are, in fact, laypersons. There are also retreat houses and religious communities that offer spiritual direction, and some directors in such situations specialize in direction for clergy. Remember that direction does not involve confession, nor should it involve revealing confidences about parishioners, which a pastor must guard. Nor should direction involve discussing congregational problems except as these may impact the minister's spiritual practices or growth in God.

Although spiritual direction is generally done one-on-one, group spiritual direction is also possible with clergy serving as directors for one another. Such groups must be thoughtfully structured and some preparatory work completed before the members of the group, in essence, become directors for one another.

Good spiritual directors, especially in rural areas, may be hard to find. Some clergy travel quite a distance for direction. Nevertheless, if you or your parishioners cannot find a spiritual director, all is not lost.

IF A SUITABLE DIRECTOR IS UNAVAILABLE

Regardless of whether or not one can find a suitable director, the goals of spiritual direction are important for anyone who is actively seeking to be found by God: (1) accountability, (2) discernment of God's action, (3) appropriate response to God's action, and (4) encouragement and prayer support. But it is not always possible to find a suitable director. What other steps can someone take to try to gain the advantages of direction when a director cannot be found?

Even if a compatible spiritual director is available, and especially if one is not, a "soul friend," or spiritual companion, can be of immense value. A soul friend is someone who can

listen compassionately and nonjudgmentally to what is happening with you spiritually. The soul friend is someone who
can pray with you when you need prayers, someone who can
share your joys and sorrows on your pilgrimage. The difference
between a soul friend and a spiritual director is that a director
generally has more training and experience in spirituality and
often will know of resources, such as books, workshops,
and prayer techniques, that might assist a particular directee.
The director can and should tailor advice to the specific
temperament and life situation of the directee, and the director can do so because of having training and experience on
which to draw in fashioning such advice. The soul friend is
more of a good listener, a compassionate sounding board, but
does not offer some of the "extras" that might come with a
spiritual director.

We are not meant to travel our spiritual journey alone. A
spiritual companion who does nothing more than listen to
and pray with you can help you to clarify how God is acting in
your life and how you might respond appropriately in order to
cooperate most effectively with God.

Reading also is often helpful. You can read spiritual classics,
such as the works of Teresa of Avila or John of the Cross, or
you might read works that express their teachings in more
contemporary language, such as those by Susan Muto. Your
pattern of life will suggest other readings, as will your ministry
and theological orientation.

And, as always, worship with a faith community is a
powerful aid in gaining strength for spiritual growth.
Unfortunately, the pastor's responsibilities during worship
services may prevent adequate time for him or her to reflect.
Perhaps you could spend a few minutes of quiet time before a
service reflecting on God's special presence in the worshiping
community and asking for strength and guidance in using

the service to help you and your congregation to grow more into God.

If you pray about finding a spiritual director, God may bring you in contact with one, or with a person who can serve as one even if that person never has thought of himself or herself as a spiritual director. It is, after all, the Holy Spirit who is doing the real work in direction. Flee from any director who claims to have the expertise to tell you what you need to do to grow into the life of God.

Always remember that whether you find a spiritual director or not, God will never abandon you. The Holy Sprit seeks to transform you into what all human beings are called to become, God's lovers—united to God in intimacy and grace, sharing in divine life, coming to know God as God knows us.

11

AIDS TO CLERGY
SPIRITUALITY

*P*ASTORAL ACCOUNTABILITY

Pastors generally are accountable to several constituencies. Most congregations have internal oversight boards with varying degrees of authority. Unless a pastor is serving a non-denominational church, he or she may also have to report to denominational executives. Accountability is a two-edged sword. It can help us remain constant in what we believe we are supposed to be doing, or it can distract us from what we think we should be doing by forcing us to spend time and energy trying to meet goals that are set by others but are not the ones we consider most important.

I will talk more about the interaction between minister and denomination later, but one goal of most, if not all, denominations is growth. This may be expressed as increasing the number of decisions for Christ, or adding to the membership rolls, or increasing average Sunday attendance. When the "boss" wants something, the boss usually gets it, or at least the appearance of it. In the secular world, this desire to please the boss sometimes leads to tragedy, such as the *Challenger* disaster in 1986, when a space shuttle exploded, resulting in the loss of seven lives. Investigations showed that engineers' warnings about system safety had been ignored in order to meet the goals set by management.

But pressure does not come always from superiors. It can come from the congregation itself, which places demands on the minister that the minister feels compelled to meet or produces conflicting demands that no one could meet. Ministers also may create demands for themselves, particularly if they want to create a record that will lead to advancement.

But the one "boss" to whom the minister is truly responsible, the only one that matters in terms of personal integrity and eternity, is Jesus Christ. Any minister who is not following where Jesus is leading is in grave spiritual danger. For the fact remains that each minister is called by Jesus first and foremost to do his work. An ordained minister knows, or should know, in his or her heart what Christ wants. It is to Christ that we are all ultimately accountable.

If we are doing what we believe God wants us to be doing, we must leave the rest to God. Almost every minister preaches that what God wants is fidelity, not success. But not all ministers practice what they preach, because the need to keep favor with the congregation, the desire to advance within the denomination, or the lure of success as the world views success is too strong to ignore. More than one minister has lost a pulpit by preaching faithfully what the congregation did not want to hear. There is the extreme example of Nazi Germany, where those courageous pastors who preached against Hitler wound up in concentration camps or, like Dietrich Bonhoeffer, were executed, while those who went along became silent accomplices of Nazi tyranny.

A minister must, therefore, be accountable primarily to Christ according to what he or she believes in conscience that Christ is asking. It is to what we believe Christ demands of us that we must be faithful, not to what others may be clamoring for. In the struggle to avoid deceiving ourselves through rationalizations or illusions, accountability to others in Christ is a powerful aid in preserving faithfulness to Christ and in clarifying what Christ asks of us and how we should respond to his call.

One such means to accountability, spiritual direction, was discussed in the last chapter. We now turn to other aids.

SUPPORT GROUPS FOR CLERGY

A support group can be an immense help in keeping clergy focused and accountable to their heartfelt priorities. Clergy support groups are groups of clergy who meet regularly to discuss individual issues in their lives and ministries in a supportive and confidential environment. Such support groups should generally consist only of clergy, with the possible exception of the facilitator, since clergy can best understand and relate to the issues that other clergy face.

Clergy may be reluctant to become part of such a support group for several reasons:

• They are afraid that what they say in the group, or even their need for a support group, will get back to their denominational executives and be used against them.

• They believe that they are in competition with other clergy, and it will hurt their image if they reveal their problems to those with whom they are competing.

• They think that they do not have time to devote to a support group, because their calendars are so full and the support group is a low priority.

• Obtaining a competent facilitator for a group, usually a mental health care professional with some understanding of the ordained ministry, requires an expense that clergy do not think they can afford and that might not be covered by their health insurance.

• A pastor feels that he or she is doing well mentally and spiritually and has no need of a support group.

Denominational executives should encourage clergy to use support groups and should provide the necessary funding for them to do so. Moreover, they must provide full assurances that support groups exist independently of the denominational lines of authority, and so whatever takes place in a group remains totally within the group. They should make it clear that instead of being a sign of weakness, taking part in a clergy support group is a sign of strength, as members of groups are confident enough to seek support and assistance in their difficult work.

That clergy feel themselves in competition with other clergy is itself a sign of spiritual distress. Unfortunately, this sense of competition is not rare, particularly when denominational goals are numerically measurable. Then the clergy are struggling to get the best numbers or are downgraded for numbers that are deemed unsuccessful. It would be best, of course, if denominations did not, even unintentionally, put clergy in such a position, but clergy who do feel stressed because of denominational pressures ought to have a support group in which they can clarify their priorities and can know that they do not have to bear their burdens alone.

Each clergy support group will probably work most productively if it has a facilitator. The facilitator can be from the laity or the clergy, but in any case should be a trained mental health professional—social worker, licensed counselor, psychiatrist, or the like—who is not directly related to any of the ministries represented. The facilitator's role is not to be the group's psychotherapist, but rather, to ask appropriate questions that draw the participants out and help them to clarify their issues and responses. The facilitator keeps order within the group, such as preventing any one person from dominating the conversation and reminding the group of proper protocol when an inappropriate comment is made. The facilitator reminds the group of its purpose and encourages members to better participation if the group seems to be losing its focus. Finally, the facilitator identifies symptoms of stress-related tension, anxiety, or depression and helps defuse these symptoms at an early stage, before they manifest themselves as more serious problems.

Support groups can meet as often as the members deem necessary, but once a month is usually sufficient unless the group has so many members that once a month would not provide an adequate chance for each individual to receive adequate time. If a group is that large, however, it is probably better to divide it into smaller groups that could function satisfactorily with monthly meetings. The more frequently the group meets, the less likely clergy are to be willing to join it. Those who are members must, of course, make regular attendance one of their highest priorities.

Those who join should be willing to be open about the issues they are struggling with, to listen carefully to others talking about their own issues, and to be compassionate and nonjudgmental in responding to whatever others say, including any comments and advice offered to them.

Are there those who do not need a support group, because all they would do in the group is talk about how good life is and how well ministry is going? Perhaps, but I have yet to meet someone who, once he or she is willing to trust someone who will listen, does not own up to problems that would benefit from being processed in a support group.

SPIRITUAL COMPANIONS
Spiritual direction and support groups are clergy aids that we have looked at thus far. A spiritual companion is someone

who, although not a spiritual director, is a compassionate listener and a trusted friend. A spiritual companion, however, is more than a friend. A spiritual companion is someone to whom you feel free to reveal the deepest yearnings of your heart, knowing that you will not be betrayed. This is someone who will pray with you and speak frankly when a candid opinion is needed. For this reason, rarely is a spiritual companion someone in a position of authority over the other person, because the power relationship would interfere with the ability of both persons to open themselves freely to each other.

A spiritual companion differs from a spiritual director in the following ways:

- The spiritual director is someone who has the training and/or experience to be able to suggest prayer techniques, workshops, books, and so forth that might be helpful in light of what the director knows about you. The spiritual companion is more of a good listener who generally does not ask as many questions or make the suggestions that a director would offer.

- You meet with a spiritual director at regular intervals and by appointment. A spiritual companion is someone whom you can often speak to over coffee at a meeting arranged on the spur of the moment.

- A spiritual director is often seen as an authority figure. The relationship with a spiritual companion is one of friendship.

- You can be a spiritual companion to someone who also is a spiritual companion to you. It is less usual, and probably inadvisable, for a directee to also direct his or her own director.

You are fortunate if you find a good spiritual director, support group, or spiritual companion. Count yourself truly blessed if you find all three.

RETREATS AND TIME AWAY

A retreat is a time to pray and reflect, away from the business and cares of the ministry, on your pattern of life, your relationship with God, and how you are responding to God's call to faithful service.

A retreat should not be used primarily as an opportunity to relax, read, or get additional education. There are substantial differences between a workshop, which is generally associated with continuing education, and a retreat, in which the emphasis is on silence, prayer, and introspection.

There are two types of retreats, guided and unguided. In a guided retreat, a spiritual director works with the retreatant, meeting at least daily during the retreat to help the retreatant clarify and respond to what God desires. The director may also suggest readings for reflection or questions to answer at the next meeting.

On the other hand, a director may suggest that the retreatant do no reading or study, thus forcing the retreatant to confront the feelings and thoughts that come during long periods of silence. This strategy is often useful with a retreatant who tends to intellectualize or rationally analyze spiritual issues. The idea is to get the retreatant out of the "head" and into the "heart," that is, more in touch with his or her feelings. Intellectualizing can amount to running away or disguising the real spiritual issues that we must confront if God is to work most effectively in and through us.

At an unguided retreat, the retreatant sets the agenda, deciding when and how to pray and on what questions to reflect. He or she may decide ahead of time what spiritual issues to meditate on during the retreat or may simply go without an agenda, asking the Holy Spirit to be the guide.

Silence is a critical component of any retreat, whether guided or unguided. Our society is plagued by noise that distracts us from the still, small voice of God within. People often do not even go for walks anymore without wearing headsets to listen to music or books on tape. Through noise and other distractions we can isolate our own environment from other human beings, thus failing to perceive what we ought to see or hear for our own spiritual welfare as well as that of others.

In silence we are more apt to encounter both God and our own demons, demons that we would rather avoid, demons that we pretend do not make their home in us. Each human being is a complex mix of angels and demons, good and evil. St. Paul was bitterly aware of this as he cried out in anguish, *"The good that I want to do I do not do, but the evil that I do not want to do, that is what I do"* (Romans 7:19).

Virtually every man and woman has developed strong defenses against their dark side. Virtually all of us have constructed illusions and worldviews that enable us to suppress parts of ourselves that we are too afraid or too ashamed to face. But we also profess that all things are known to God. We can hide from ourselves, but we cannot hide from God.

In order to break down our defenses so that God can build on their ruins, we must often spend a week or more in silence. It is easy to do a one-day retreat, even with expert guidance, and still avoid the issues that we most need to address. It is much less easy to spend eight days in silence in the presence of God and avoid what God demands that we address, not to punish us but to purify us so that we can belong more completely to God.

This is not to imply that a retreat, any more than spiritual direction, is intended to be psychotherapy. If a serious psychopathology exists, it needs to be treated by a mental health care professional, not by a retreat director. Rather, now, I am speaking about spiritual pathologies and illusions that need to be revealed by the light of God and purified in the fire of the Holy Spirit. I am talking about understanding our true priorities and realigning them, when necessary, to make God our highest priority. I am talking about the self-understanding and conversion that only God can bring about in us if we will allow God to do so.

A retreat can be an environment in which God acts powerfully in our lives, but it is unlikely to be so if it is treated merely as an extension of our busy lives in a different location. A pastor who brings along a laptop computer on retreat to work on a sermon and stay in touch with the church office is not on retreat, but rather, is making the retreat center a branch office of the church. It takes discipline and desire to make a good retreat, to block out one's calendar for a week or more, to make oneself unavailable except in the case of a dire emergency. I strongly recommend that every pastor go on a retreat annually or at least every other year.

SABBATICALS AND CONTINUING EDUCATION

I was fortunate recently to have had a three-month sabbatical sponsored by my diocese. During that time I was able to make a week-long silent retreat at a Trappist monastery, pursue continuing education opportunities, visit other churches— including those of other denominations, both to worship and to get ideas that might prove useful for my own church— and be involved in other activities that would have been impossible had I not been freed from my usual responsibilities.

The sabbatical also gave my congregation an opportunity to experience the clergy who supplied in my absence and to take responsibility for the day-to-day operation of the church and for ministering to one another. They were glad to have me back, but I was proud of them for the outstanding job they did in keeping things running smoothly while I was gone. In addition to making sure that the sick were visited and the ministry of the church continued, they even initiated a new program in the church.

As was the case with my own sabbatical, sabbaticals can be useful for both the pastor and the church. For the pastor, a sabbatical provides rest and recreation as well as time for reflection and study, a time to "charge the batteries" and gain new ideas. It is also a time during which a pastor has adequate time to think about priorities and programs, both personal and congregational, in order to generate new ideas or reinvigorate old ones. For the congregation, it enables them to care for one another without depending on the pastor and to make sure that their church—and it is their church, not the pastor's—continues to operate smoothly.

Unfortunately, not all churches can afford to give sabbaticals to their clergy. My own church could not have afforded it without aid from my diocese. My diocese recognizes the need for sabbaticals—three months after five years at the same church—and is willing to help fund them when the church cannot. A Methodist minister told me that his judicatory allows clergy a one-year sabbatical every ten years, but the ministers have to fund it themselves. This often means that a sabbatical is not feasible, or that the minister must take another paying position to make ends meet, which can interfere with some of the benefits that a sabbatical is supposed to confer.

My diocese's choice of three months for the length of a sabbatical was not based on economics, but rather, on research that indicates that if a pastor is gone from the church longer than three months, ties to the congregation may be broken and he or she will be returning to a strange church. Some pastors may be afraid to be gone even three months from their congregations because they are certain that the church will

collapse without them. Pastors who feel this way should examine whether their congregation has become overly dependent
on them, or whether they themselves have an inflated sense of
their importance to their flock. The church is, after all, God's
church. Any excessive human dependence, even, or especially,
on the pastor, may indicate serious pathologies that need to be
named and healed.

Continuing education should also be a regular source of
growth and renewal for clergy, helping them to expand their
horizons and bring new ideas and skills into their ministries.
Attending denominational meetings, however, generally does
not qualify as continuing education.

A pastor, particularly one at a small church, sometimes has
to make work to fill forty hours a week. But no pastor should
make work. A pastor's entire life should be one of prayer and
spiritual growth. The pastor who feels compelled to be "doing"
something every moment will neglect the "being" portion of
spiritual life. If we are not able to be present to God, we will
have a much harder time being present to those who most
need our love and compassion, which ought to be God's love
and compassion. No congregation should begrudge its pastor
the time needed to grow spiritually by the grace of God, and
no pastor should begrudge himself or herself that time either.

If we recognize that our lives must be constant affirmations
of our desire to grow into the life of God and of our openness
to allow God to transform us, we will become better servants
of God and better pastors to our people. If we cannot recognize this truth, which should be the cornerstone of our
ministry, then we, and our congregations and communities,
will be the worse for it.

12

SPECIAL CLERGY
SPIRITUAL ISSUES

ERVANT LEADERSHIP
All clergy are symbols of Christ. They do not have the choice of whether or not to be such symbols. To many people, they are. It is not that people confuse them with Christ (although some clergy may confuse themselves with Christ!). Rather, many people judge Christianity by the actions and lives of its most visible representatives. Clergy, above all, must try to reflect Christ in their lives and ministries as much as, or more than, they preach him in their sermons.

Christ himself taught us that his was a servant ministry. Whoever would be first must be the servant of all. Even though Jesus was God incarnate, he emptied himself and took the form of a servant, even stooping to wash the feet of his disciples before the Last Supper to impress on them the importance of servant ministry.

Clergy are in a position of leadership in the church. So their leadership must be servant leadership. But what does servant leadership imply, and for whom are the clergy servants?

Clergy are first and foremost servants of Christ. To be a servant implies service to a master, and our master is the Lord Jesus Christ. First and foremost, we must conform our will to the will of Christ as best we can discern it. Christ expressly taught his disciples to exercise servant leadership, so in keeping with that mandate, we must be servant leaders as well. But what does servant leadership require? Here I offer six suggestions, using Christ's behavior as a model.

First, we prepare others for ministry. Christ prepared his disciples for ministry by teaching them and by sending them out to preach and to heal. After his resurrection, he could have chosen to stay on earth, operating as the head of the church, but he chose to ascend to heaven, turning his work over to his disciples. He sent the Holy Spirit to give them courage, wisdom, and power from God, but he did not stay around to look over their shoulder. First he prepared them to continue his work, and then he left them.

A great temptation for those of us in the clergy is to believe that we must control and direct what the members of our congregation do and believe. We are the ones who are anointed, trained, learned in Scripture, ordained of God to protect and lead the sheep. We may come to believe that ministry is more a matter of control, like herding sheep, than it is of preparing people to be disciples of Jesus and allowing them to become servant ministers themselves. Christ taught and he empowered, but he did not control.

Second, we listen to the needs and ideas of others in making plans with, rather than imposing our own vision on, our congregation. Clergy provide positive leadership and even a vision, when appropriate, to inspire a congregation to action, but they must recognize that they are still members of the body of Christ, and all parts must work together in harmony for the body to function properly.

Third, we are willing to take on any task, even a menial task, so that the work of Christ may be accomplished. There is no work of Christ that we should be unwilling to do because we see it as being beneath us or as something fit only for the laity. One way to inspire service in others is to set an example, just as Jesus did when he washed his disciples' feet.

Fourth, our lives are examples of sacrificial love. Christ commanded his followers to love others as they have first been loved. We have been loved with a sacrificial love, a love that was willing to give up even life itself to bring the lost into the kingdom. We must be willing to put aside, if need be, our desires and interests in order to be Christ to others. We all have persons in our congregations whom we would be happy to see transfer to another church. We are to love even those who annoy us most with the love that Christ displayed to all, even those who crucified him. "Father, forgive them, because they do not know what they are doing" (Luke 23:34). This is the love with which we are to reach out to everyone.

Fifth, we speak the truth in love. Pastors are often tempted to "go with the flow" or "go along to get along." But when the truth needs to be told, when unpopular views need to be expressed because they contain the message of Christ that church members need to hear, we must be willing to speak out. If the churches of Germany had been willing to stand fast against Nazism, who knows how many lives would have been saved? If the churches of the South had refused to condone slavery, perhaps the Civil War would not have had to occur. If a man who is the biggest giver in our congregation is leading an openly immoral life, do we have the courage to confront him in private to urge him to repent? There is no falsehood in God. Jesus Christ is the truth. We must be willing to speak the truth in love whenever our conscience demands it.

Sixth, we listen for the Holy Spirit speaking to us through others. Not only must we allow others to express their views about the work of the church, but we must also recognize that the Holy Spirit may speak to us through the least in our flock, and even through those not of our flock. Ministers expect others to listen to their views of what God wants, yet often they themselves are unwilling to listen to others who may have words of wisdom for them. We must listen to what others say to us with prayer and discernment, as if these words come from Jesus himself.

COMMUNITY AND SPIRITUALITY
Christianity is, and always will be, a religion of community. Those who claim that they can get along well without belonging to a community of faith are cheating themselves out of one of the most powerful spiritual aids that Jesus gave us.

I keep repeating that we are all members of the body of Christ and that we all share in the ministry of Christ, each individually according to the particular call and gifts that God has given. We need one another not only to carry out the work that God has given us to do collectively, but also to support and pray for one another as each one of us carries out that work. Here are but four of the spiritual benefits of community:

A fuller presence of Christ. Jesus tells us that where two or three are gathered in his name, he will be there with them (Matthew 18:20). He is present, of course, in each one of us as individual members of his body, but he is present in an even more powerful way whenever two or three or more members gather. When we worship as the people of God, we are more than individuals praying privately. We are the church, and in a real though mysterious way, the whole church, in all times and places, is present at our liturgy, the "work of the people." In community, we are far more than the sum of our parts.

A fuller presence of the Holy Spirit. Each of us is a temple of the Holy Spirit, but also, each of us is an instrument of the Holy Spirit for one another, often speaking words that others need to hear, whether they be words of consolation, compassion, wisdom, prayer, or even contradiction. As we come together in the love of Jesus Christ as members of his body, we are more likely to experience the power and gifts of the Spirit than we do as individuals. There is, of course, a time for being alone, as in silent retreats and private prayer, but there is a time to be together as well so that the Spirit may act in us together. At his ascension, Jesus told his disciples to pray and wait for the coming of the Holy Spirit. They did not go off as individuals. They came together as a group and prayed as a group, and the Holy Spirit descended on them as they prayed as a body.

A *sharing of gifts and ministries*. An ocean liner could not function if every member of its crew did the same job, say, that of the purser. There would be no one to clean the cabins, prepare and serve the food, provide entertainment, or even keep the engines running and the ship on course. As a community, we enjoy more gifts and a greater representation of the work of Jesus Christ than any individual other than he himself can provide. As a group, we can do far more than any one of us can do individually.

A *sharing of experiences and wisdom*. The collective experience and wisdom of a healthy group is generally more valuable than the experience and wisdom of any one of its members. Unfortunately, with an unhealthy group, destructive tendencies can be reinforced, as when a mob loots and burns even though no member of the mob would engage in such behavior alone. As pastors, we must try to channel the energies of our congregations in constructive ways. I have found that when a congregation is healthy, its unhealthy and potentially divisive members either leave or are isolated by the healthy members who do not let them exercise any real influence in the church.

A healthy community requires a healthy spirituality on the part of both the pastor and the majority of the members. A spiritually healthy pastor can often serve as an instrument of healing for a sick community, but a sick pastor can infect a healthy community. This is one of the principal reasons why a pastor must have a strong and healthy spirituality.

WORSHIP AND SPIRITUALITY

Communal worship generally reflects the spiritual health of the pastor and the congregation. Worship should enable the congregation to encounter God in a real and powerful way and strengthen them for their work outside of the church. In this day of dwindling numbers of churchgoers and a strong desire for "better numbers," a pastor may be tempted to make the service more "entertaining" and "relevant."

I am not suggesting that services should be boring and irrelevant, but our services, like our teachings, must speak the truth in love. Each denomination has its own ethos to which it must be true. Many churches today do their best to disguise their affiliation with a denomination because such affiliations are not deemed popular with the younger generations. They sometimes break with their traditions, and not infrequently their theology, to try to create services that will keep the attention of the multimedia generation.

Each church, like each pastor, must ask itself who they are. What is their spirituality? What do they truly believe? What is their vision? Their worship must reflect their spirituality, their beliefs, and their vision.

A pastor might well invite someone she trusts who is unchurched, perhaps even offering him a small stipend, to attend a typical worship service. This visitor would be asked to make a written record of his impressions. Did he feel welcome? Did he sense a special reverence in the congregation toward the service? Did he gain any special insights about the congregation and the pastor from the service, and if so, what were they? Did the service seem to have a coherence, a unity that made it easy to follow from beginning to end, or did it seem like various unrelated bits and pieces pasted together? Was there any underlying theme or message conveyed by the service? Was he better able to understand what it means to be a member of this church and what would be expected of him if he were to join?

These are questions that the members themselves should be asked from time to time. Worship must bring us all into contact with the living God. It must "recharge our spiritual batteries" and give us strength to go on at times when we feel like throwing in the towel. Our worship must remind us whose we are, what God has done for us, and what God expects of us. Our worship must repeatedly remind us of the power and the love of God.

Each denomination has developed services that embody its tradition and unique ethos within the glorious quilt that is Christianity. While the desire for unity in worship and theology is the dream of many, it is just that—a dream. For all denominations to be united as one, the common denominator required to form the foundation for union would have to be so insipid as to cause the loss of more than would be gained. We are one in the Spirit and one in the Lord, but we are divided in how we express our lives in Christ. We ought not disguise who we think we are, nor carelessly throw away those traditions of which we are the guardians.

Worship should challenge the worshipers. If God is present, that presence itself should inspire awe. A church is not a movie theater or a sports stadium. It is holy ground where God and the people of God come together. This is the essence of worship that must never be diluted, even if the service itself is modified. If the service is modified, any changes must be made in order to enhance the encounter with God.

If we sell our spiritual birthrights, even for the seemingly tasty pottage of numerical growth, we will be left with nothing to hand down to those who follow us. It is primarily in worship that we celebrate and express our spirituality. We separate the two only at great peril to our integrity and the integrity of our churches.

RELATIONSHIP TO THE DENOMINATION

As noted above, a number of congregations affiliated with a denomination prefer to downplay or even disguise that affiliation. The number of persons attending nonaffiliated or independent congregations has grown, while the numbers in mainline denominations generally are trending downward.

A denomination, however, should be the expression of a religious heritage. Each denomination, like each person, has a history that stretches into the past. The heritage includes the specific doctrinal emphases and manner of worship that define the denomination. A church that denies its denominational heritage or attempts to disguise it so as to be more "inclusive" risks losing its identity, and perhaps its soul, because it is not living in truth.

Nevertheless, many denominations today are torn by divisive struggles that pit member against member. Factions fight for control of the denomination's agenda. The issue may be ordination of women, same-sex unions, support of "liberal" seminaries, or something else. Some churches are questioning whether they want to continue their affiliation with their denomination. I do not presume to have the answers to such thorny problems, problems that wrack my own national Episcopal Church, but I do stress that a pastor and a church each must be sure of their own spirituality. Spirituality gives identity and direction. A pattern of life gives discipline and opens the soul to God's transforming grace. A church that has a clear vision of itself and a spirituality that is understood and shared by its members will stand strong against the winds that buffet it. They, like Luther, can declare, "Here I stand. I cannot do otherwise."

But developing a spirituality requires prayerful thought, whether for an individual or for a congregation. If the congregation and pastor are faithful to their denominational heritage, their spirituality will reflect that heritage, or at least be consistent with it. If they find themselves at odds with that heritage, then prayer and patient reflection are needed to discern the implications of this conflict and how to resolve it.

We live in a world in which history and tradition too often are little valued. The danger of forgetting or ignoring our traditions and doctrinal uniqueness is that we will lose the map that guides us on our journey. There may be such a thing as a "generic Christian denomination," but I am not certain what creed, if any, it would use to define its membership, and I certainly do not know what its worship would be like. Generic worship most likely would be directed at arousing the emotions rather than strengthening pilgrims for the journey; at making people feel good rather than making them uncomfortable with the parts of their lives that do not yet belong to Christ. Generic items may be the cheapest, but there is no such thing as cheap grace. Grace is costly to God—the high price of the death of Christ on our account—and we are asked to give nothing less than our lives to realize the potential that grace brings us.

Nor is there such a thing as a "generic spirituality." Our spirituality is unique; it defines our individual relationship with, and our personal search for, God. A generic spirituality, a spirituality that suits everyone, is no spirituality at all. Christ asked his first disciples, "Who do you say that I am?" He asks us the same question, but inherent in that question now is the question "Who do say that you are?" Our answer, flowing from prayer and the depths of our being, is our spirituality.

THE ROLE OF THE LAITY

A division usually is made between clergy and laity. The clergy are the ordained, the anointed, the chosen leaders of the congregations. The laity are those whom the clergy lead. There must be leaders in any organization, but as we have seen, servant leadership implies that the ordained leadership must empower the laity to exercise ministry themselves. In other words, the leaders lead not by demanding obedience to their directives but in ways that inspire and enable the laity to realize and exercise their own talents and gifts in the service of God.

Clergy can also help the laity to define their own spiritualities by teaching about spirituality and modeling in their own lives how to live out a spirituality. They can also encourage the laity to develop a pattern of life that carries them through the times when they are not in church, so they can make growth into God a conscious part of their lives.

VULNERABILITY

Vulnerability means that clergy do not build defensive walls between themselves and those they lead. My own experience leads me to believe that clergy have a difficult time being vulnerable. They are afraid to expose themselves as possibly being weak, ignorant, or sinful, having fears and problems not unlike those of their parishioners.

A minister may be afraid that revealing a weakness will reduce his or her ability to lead. Moreover, because parishioners generally expect their ministers to be models of how a

Christian should live, and assume that persons who live good Christian lives will be at peace and happy, they are disturbed when their clergy are troubled or confess that they themselves often feel that God is distant or has abandoned them altogether.

But the rock on which the church is built is not the clergy; it is Jesus Christ. The local church likewise must be founded on this rock. The local church is a "hospital for sinners" and a place in which to encounter God and Jesus Christ through worship and through the love and support that should be present if the community is spiritually sound even though its members are still in need of healing.

On the first Sunday of each month at my small church I offer the laying on of hands and anointing for healing to anyone wishing to receive it. Although this practice was begun a number of years ago, almost all of those present still come forward to receive what for Episcopalians is a sacrament. Whether one considers this ritual a sacrament or not, it is found in Scripture and is a means to ask God to heal those illnesses and wounds from which every human being suffers.

The ritual is powerful and moving each time we have it. Some people cry, while others have said that they experienced healing. But always, God is present then in a palpable way. As the one administering the sacrament, I could stand aloof and not admit my own need for healing. But after the last member of the congregation has been prayed for and anointed, I kneel and have several members of my congregation pray for me and anoint me with oil. I am part of the prayers for healing not just in administering a sacrament, but also in recognizing that I am in as much need of healing as my parishioners, perhaps more. By my participation I also recognize that I am not the one who is the healer. Christ is the one who heals. Each one of us, clergy and laity alike, is in need of healing, and we also can and should serve as instruments of Christ in that healing.

Clergy might believe that they can reveal their humanity only to other clergy, who understand the tensions with which they live and work. Certainly, clergy cannot reveal confidential information when they share their own concerns with parishioners, but a congregation that cannot live with a fully human pastor does not understand the mystery of the incarnation. Such a congregation would be horrified to think that the baby Jesus soiled his diapers or that a mature Jesus had body odor. They want their Christianity clean and neat, but Christianity is not clean and neat. God became a human being not because humanity was clean and neat, but because it needed to be made whole. Humanity needed a way to come to God, to share in God's life. God became a human being not because humanity had earned that privilege, but because humanity never could, of its own resources, grow into the life of God.

Clergy and laity are in this life together. The clergy have a role assigned to them by God, to serve the body of Christ in a particular way. But the role is one of service, and it is to guide their people through loving service toward what God destines them to become.

Clergy need not reveal their secret sins to their congregations any more than their members must reveal their secret sins to their clergy. We call on God for forgiveness in the name of Christ, recognizing, as Scripture tells us, that anyone who claims to be sinless is self-deceiving and false and makes God out to be a liar (1 John 1:8,10). Clergy who pretend that they are above their people are like those Christ warned about who claim to be first but wind up being last at the banquet of the Lord.

We may fool others, but we cannot fool God. To God all hearts are open and all secrets revealed. If we cut ourselves off from the support that our congregations can give us because we believe it will interfere with the support we can give them, we are fooling ourselves, and we may be jeopardizing the effectiveness of our ministries because we are cutting ourselves off from those we serve and whose love and support we need.

To truly love is to make oneself vulnerable. To open one's heart to others is to make oneself vulnerable. To ask others for love and support is to make oneself vulnerable. To admit to being human is to make oneself vulnerable. Our relationship with Jesus and those we serve demands that we take that risk.

"THE TIMES THEY ARE A-CHANGIN'"

At one time, clergy were respected and could lead because of the office they held. Now, however, they must earn respect before those they lead will trust them and accept their vision for the church.

At one time, pretty much all a church had to do was open its doors and people would fill it. Today, many churches that expanded in the boom of the 1950s sit with sanctuaries all but empty at Sunday services and Sunday school classrooms that go unused.

The younger the generation, the lower the percentage of that generation that goes to church. The old models, such as kids leaving church when they leave home and returning when they start a family, are less and less visible. Many children today have never been to any church, and neither have their parents. There is no family church for the children to return to, and in addition, they see no need for church.

Some have said that we live in a post-Christian society. Our nation is no longer overtly Christian—assuming that it ever was. People may pay lip service to Christian values, but their hearts are far from the teaching and example of Christ.

This is not altogether bad. Those who come to church now,

for the most part, really want to come to church. In a few years, those for whom the church fills a void in their lives may be the only ones in attendance. That is probably the way it was in the early church. People went to church then, even though it might cost them their lives, because they recognized that Jesus and his church offered them something that they could get only from him.

There is an adage that one often sees displayed on the signs in front of churches: "If you feel that God is no longer close to you, who moved?" Churches must try as best they can to be close to God so that those who do come to church can encounter God there. This implies that the congregation and the clergy each have a spirituality that defines them and guides their lives. Without such a spirituality, the church will drift with the tides of the times, trying this fad and that to recover what they once thought they had.

God is ever present for us, and we can realize that presence if we accept God's invitation to grow into divine life and open our hearts and souls to transforming grace. A spirituality and a pattern of life are important, perhaps indispensable, aids in this quest. We must never lose sight of our goal both as clergy and as Christians, for that goal is nothing less than God.

SELECT BIBLIOGRAPHY

Barna, George. *Real Teens: A Contemporary Snapshot of Youth Culture*. Colorado Springs: WaterBrook Press, 2001. A representative work by Barna on contemporary trends in religion. See also his *Boiling Point: It Only Takes One Degree* (Ventura, Calif.: Gospel Light, 2001) and *Baby Busters: The Disillusioned Generation* (Chicago: Northfield, 1994).

Freeman, Laurence. *Jesus: The Teacher Within*. New York: Continuum International Publishing Group, 2001. A representative work on prayer by Freeman. See also his *Time Alone with God* (with Tum Hufty; Minneapolis: Bethany House, 1999) and *Light Within: The Inner Path of Meditation* (New York: Crossroad Publishing Co., 1986).

Gemignani, Michael. *To Know God: Small Group Exercises for Spiritual Formation*. Valley Forge, Pa.: Judson Press, 2000. Possible basis for clergy spiritual formation and direction groups.

Guenther, Margaret. *Holy Listening: The Art of Spiritual Direction*. Boston: Cowley Publications, 1992. A discussion of spiritual direction by a master director and teacher.

Hall, Thelma. *Too Deep for Words: Rediscovering Lectio Divina*. Mahwah, N.J.: Paulist Press, 1988. A work generally recognized as a classic on prayer.

Jones, Alan. *Exploring Spiritual Direction*. Boston: Cowley Publications, 1999. An excellent introduction to spiritual direction by a prolific writer on the spiritual life.

SELECT BIBLIOGRAPHY

Keating, Thomas. *Open Heart, Open Mind*. New York: Continuum International Publishing Group, 1994. An excellent introduction to centering prayer.

May, Gerald. *Care of Mind, Care of Spirit: A Psychiatrist Explores Spiritual Direction*. San Francisco: HarperSanFrancisco, 1992. A discussion by a psychiatrist and spiritual director on the relationship between our human psychological makeup and our spiritual nature with practical pointers on caring for ourselves spiritually.

Merton, Thomas. *New Seeds of Contemplation*. New York: W. W. Norton, 1974. Merton is recognized as one of the modern masters of the interior life and the contemplative way.

―――. *Wisdom of the Desert*. New York: W. W. Norton, 1988. A small book with a great deal of condensed spiritual wisdom.

Nouwen, Henri. *The Way of the Heart*. New York: Ballantine, 1992. Nouwen is a recognized master of the spiritual life and one who writes with a special intimacy and eloquence. In this work, Nouwen speaks of solitude, silence, and prayer.

―――. *Genesee Diary: Report from a Trappist Monastery*. New York: Image Books, 1981. Particularly recommended for those who think that spiritual masters do not go through the same trials that ordinary folks do.

Pennington, M. Basil. *Centering Prayer*. New York: Doubleday, 1987. A representative work by Pennington on prayer, as cited in chapter 8. See also his *Lectio Divina: Renewing the Ancient Practice of Praying the Scriptures* (New York: Crossroad Publishing Co., 1998).

Rolheiser, Ronald. *The Holy Longing: Guidelines for a Christian Spirituality*. New York: Doubleday, 1999. A search for a Christian spirituality that makes sense in the modern world.

Smith, Martin. *The Word Is Very Near You: A Guide to Praying with Scripture*. Boston: Cowley Publications, 1989. A guide to lectio divina, as the title implies.

Wuthnow, Robert. *After Heaven: Spirituality in America since the 1950s*. University of California Press, 2000. A representative work by Wuthnow on the sociology of contemporary religion. See also his *The Restructuring of American Religion: Society and Faith since World War II* (Princeton, N.J.: Princeton University Press, 1990).